Congressional Research Service
Informing the legislative debate since 1914 _____

Iran Sanctions

Kenneth Katzman
Specialist in Middle Eastern Affairs

August 19, 2014

Congressional Research Service

7-5700

www.crs.gov

RS20871

Summary

Strict sanctions on Iran's key energy and financial sectors harmed Iran's economy. The economic pressure—coupled with the related June 14, 2013, election of the relatively moderate Hassan Rouhani as Iran's president—contributed to Iran's accepting a November 24, 2013, six-month interim agreement ("Joint Plan of Action," JPA) that halts expansion of its nuclear program in exchange for modest sanctions relief. On July 18, 2014, the interim agreement was extended until November 24, 2014. The economic pressure of sanctions included the following:

- Oil exports fund nearly half of Iran's government expenditures and, by late 2013, sanctions had reduced Iran's oil exports to about 1 million barrels per day—far below the 2.5 million barrels per day Iran exported during 2011.

- During 2012-2013, the loss of revenues from oil, coupled with the cut-off of Iran from the international banking system, caused a sharp drop in the value of Iran's currency, the *rial*; raised inflation to over 50%; and cut off Iran's access to most of its hard currency held outside the country. Iran's economy shrank by about 5% in 2013 as many Iranian firms reduced operations and loans became delinquent.

The JPA agreement, including the approximately $7 billion in sanctions relief during the interim period, of which $4.2 billion ($700 million per month) was access to hard currency from oil sales, began implementation on January 20, 2014, and provisions of several laws and executive orders were waived or suspended that day. The JPA extension until November 24, 2014, continues all sanctions relief provisions, including $2.8 billion in access to hard currency ($700 million per month multiplied by four months of extension).

Citing some improvements in Iran's economy and renewed international business contacts with Iran, some in Congress believe that economic pressure on Iran needs to increase to shape a final nuclear deal and ensure that the Iran sanctions architecture does not collapse. On the other hand, many economic assessments indicate that the sanctions relief of the JPA has halted further deterioration in Iran's economy but has not caused dramatic economic improvement.

Sanctions have, to some extent, slowed Iran's nuclear and missile programs and reduced its military power by hampering its acquisition of foreign technology and weaponry. However, the sanctions have not halted Iran's provision of arms to the Assad government in Syria, the Iraqi government, and to pro-Iranian factions in the Middle East. Nor have sanctions altered Iran's repression of dissent or monitoring of the Internet.

A comprehensive nuclear agreement, if reached, would undoubtedly require significant easing of U.S. and third country sanctions on Iran—particularly those sanctions imposed since 2010 that are intended primarily to compel Iran to reach a nuclear agreement. The Administration has said that sanctions relief under a comprehensive deal would be implemented stepwise as Iran fulfills the terms of an agreement. Although it might be able to act on its own authority to suspend most sanctions on Iran to implement a comprehensive deal, the Administration has said it would work with Congress on longer term sanctions relief. See also CRS Report RL32048, *Iran: U.S. Concerns and Policy Responses*, by Kenneth Katzman; CRS Report R43311, *Iran: U.S. Economic Sanctions and the Authority to Lift Restrictions*, by Dianne E. Rennack; and CRS Report R43492, *Achievements of and Outlook for Sanctions on Iran*, by Kenneth Katzman.

Contents

Overview and Objectives 1

Blocked Iranian Property and Assets 1

Executive Order 13599 Impounding Iran-Owned Assets 2

Sanctions Against Iran's Support for International Terrorism and Regional Activities 3

Sanctions Triggered by Terrorism List Designation: Ban on U.S. Aid, Arms Sales,
Dual-Use Exports, and Certain Programs for Iran 3

No Ban on U.S. Humanitarian Aid 4

Executive Order 13224: Sanctioning Terrorism Supporting Entities 4

Sanctioning Iranian Involvement in the Region 4

Ban on U.S. Trade and Investment with Iran 5

Major Provisions: What U.S.-Iran Trade Is Allowed or Prohibited? 6

Application to Foreign Subsidiaries of U.S. Firms 8

Energy and Other Sector Sanctions: Iran Sanctions Act (ISA) and Related Laws and
Executive Orders 9

The Iran Sanctions Act, Amendments, and Related Applications 9

Key "Triggers" 10

Mandate and Time Frame to Investigate ISA Violations 14

Clarification of Responsibilities: Executive Order 13574 17

Interpretations and Administration of ISA and Related Laws 17

Application to Energy Pipelines 17

Application to Crude Oil Purchases 17

Application to Natural Gas Purchases from Iran/Shah Deniz Exception 17

Application to Liquefied Natural Gas Development 18

Application to Private Financing but Not Official Credit Guarantee Agencies 18

Application to Iranian Energy Institutions/NIOC and NITC 18

Sanctions Imposed Under ISA 19

Sanctions on Oil and Other Payments to Iran's Central Bank 20

Implementation: Exemptions Issued 21

Sanctions on Paying Iran with Hard Currency 22

Proliferation-Related Sanctions 23

Iran-Iraq Arms Nonproliferation Act and Iraq Sanctions Act 23

Iran-North Korea-Syria Nonproliferation Act 24

Executive Order 13382 25

Foreign Aid Restrictions for Suppliers of Iran 25

Sanctions on "Countries of Diversion Concern" 25

Financial/Banking Sanctions 26

Early Efforts: Targeted Financial Measures 27

CISADA: Sanctioning Foreign Banks That Conduct Transactions with Iran 27

Implementation of Section 104: Sanctions Imposed 28

Iran Designated a Money-Laundering Jurisdiction 28

Promoting Divestment 29

Sanctions and Sanctions Exemptions to Support Democratic Change/Civil Society in Iran 29

Expanding Internet and Communications Freedoms 30

Sanctions and Administrative Actions Against Iran's Internet Censorship 30

Measures to Sanction Human Rights Abuses and Promote the Opposition 31
    Sanctions Against Iranian Human Rights Abusers and Related Equipment 31
    Sanctions Against Iranian Broadcasting and Profiteers.. 32
    Separate Visa Ban... 32
U.N. Sanctions 33
International Implementation and Compliance.. 34
    Europe 34
    Japan and Korean Peninsula.. 36
        North Korea.. 36
    India... 36
    Pakistan 37
    China and Russia 38
    Turkey/South Caucasus 39
        Caucasus: Azerbaijan, Armenia, and Georgia 39
    Persian Gulf and Iraq 40
    Afghanistan.. 41
    Latin America 41
    Africa... 42
    World Bank Loans 42
    Private-Sector Cooperation and Compliance... 45
        Foreign Firms Reportedly Remaining in the Iran Market 47
Effectiveness of Sanctions on Iran.. 48
    Effect on Iran's Nuclear Program Decisions and Capabilities 48
    Effects on Iran's Strategic Programs and Regional Influence 49
    General Political Effects.. 50
    Human Rights-Related Effects 50
    Economic Effects... 51
        Iran's Mitigation Efforts.. 53
    Effect on Energy Sector Long-Term Development 53
        Effect on Gasoline Availability and Importation.. 59
    Humanitarian Effects/Air Safety 61
Sanctions Easings and Debate Following November 24, 2013, Nuclear Deal 61
    Temporary Sanctions Relief in the JPA 62
    Permanent Sanctions Easing?.. 63
    Possible Additional Sanctions 64
        H.R. 850 and S. 1881 64
    Other Possible U.S. and International Sanctions 66

Tables

Table 1. ISA Sanctions Determinations 20
Table 2. Top Energy Buyers From Iran and Reductions... 23
Table 3. Summary of Provisions of U.N. Resolutions on Iran Nuclear Program (1737,
    1747, 1803, and 1929) 33
Table 4. Comparison Between U.S., U.N., and EU and Allied Country Sanctions 43

Table 5. Post-1999 Major Investments/Major Development Projects
in Iran's Energy Sector 55

Table 6. Firms That Sold Gasoline to Iran 60

Table 7. Entities Sanctioned Under U.N. Resolutions and
U.S. Laws and Executive Orders 68

Contacts

Author Contact Information 79

Overview and Objectives

U.S. sanctions have been a major feature of U.S. Iran policy since Iran's 1979 Islamic revolution, but U.N. and worldwide bilateral sanctions on Iran are a relatively recent (post-2006) development. Many of the U.S. sanctions reinforce U.N. and multilateral sanctions put in place in recent years by European and some Asian countries. Successive Administrations have sought to ensure that U.S. sanctions do not hamper cooperation with key international partners whose support is needed to isolate Iran.

The objectives of U.S. sanctions have evolved over time. In the mid-1980s, U.S. sanctions were intended to try to compel Iran to cease supporting acts of terrorism and to limit Iran's strategic power in the Middle East more generally. Since the mid-1990s, U.S. sanctions have focused increasingly on persuading or compelling Iran to limit the scope of its nuclear program to ensure purely civilian use. Since 2006, and particularly since 2010, the international community has joined U.S. sanctions in pursuit of that goal.

This report analyzes U.S. and international sanctions against Iran and, in so doing, provides examples, based on a wide range of open source reporting, of companies and countries that conduct business with Iran. CRS has no way to independently corroborate any of the reporting on which these examples are based and no mandate to assess whether any entity is complying with U.S. or international sanctions against Iran.

Implementation of some of the sanctions is subject to interpretation. On November 13, 2012, the Administration published in the *Federal Register* (Volume 77, Number 219) "Policy Guidance" explaining how it implements many of the sanctions discussed below.[1] The guidance also sets out examples of specific products and chemicals that are included in the definitions of such terms as "petroleum," "petroleum products," and "petrochemical products" that are used in the laws and executive orders discussed below.

The sections below are grouped according to functional theme, and presented in the chronological order in which these themes have emerged in U.S. sanctions policy toward Iran. It should be noted, however, that most U.S. sanctions against Iran have had multiple objectives and were enacted to address different perceived threats from Iran at the same time. It is so indicated if a certain sanctions provision is being suspended as a consequence of the JPA, the duration of which is from January 20, 2014, to July 20, 2014, unless extended by mutual agreement or replaced by a comprehensive agreement.

Blocked Iranian Property and Assets

Some U.S. sanctions began at the time of the U.S.-Iran hostage crisis of 1979-1981 in the form of Carter Administration executive orders blocking Iranian assets held in the United States. The assets were unblocked by subsequent Orders when the crisis was resolved in early 1981 under the "Algiers Accords." Iranian leaders continue to assert that the United States is holding Iranian assets dating from that time.

---

[1] http://www.regulations.gov/#!documentDetail;D=DOS_FRDOC_0001-2175.

The Algiers Accords established a "U.S.-Iran Claims Tribunal" at the Hague continues to arbitrate cases resulting from the 1980 break in relations and freezing of some of Iran's assets. Major cases yet to be decided center on hundreds of Foreign Military Sales (FMS) cases between the United States and the Shah's regime, which Iran claims it paid for but were unfulfilled. A reported $400 million in proceeds from the resale of that equipment was placed in a DOD FMS account and may remain in this escrow account, although DOD has not provided CRS with a precise balance. In addition, about $50 million in Iranian diplomatic property and accounts remains blocked—this amount includes proceeds from rents received on the former Iranian embassy in Washington, DC, and 10 other properties in several states, along with related bank accounts.[2] Including Iranian assets blocked under Executive Order 1399 of February 2010, discussed below, about $1.95 billion in Iranian assets is blocked, according to the 2013 "Terrorist Assets Report."

Other past financial disputes include the mistaken U.S. shoot-down on July 3, 1988, of an Iranian Airbus passenger jet (Iran Air flight 655), for which the United States paid Iran $61.8 million in compensation ($300,000 per wage earning victim, $150,000 per nonwage earner) for the 248 Iranians killed. The United States did not compensate Iran for the airplane itself, although officials involved in the negotiations told CRS in November 2012 that the United States later arranged to provide a substitute, used aircraft to Iran.

In late 2009, the U.S. Attorney for the Southern District of New York seized the assets of the Assa Company, a UK-chartered entity. Assa allegedly was maintaining the interests of Bank Melli in an office building in New York City. An Iranian foundation, the Alavi Foundation, allegedly is an investor in the building.

Some of Iran's assets have been held against legal judgments ordering Iran to compensate U.S. victims of Iranian-backed terrorism. Among recent terrorism victim judgments, on July 6, 2012, a U.S. federal judge ordered Iran to pay $813 million to the families of the 241 U.S. soldiers killed in the October 23, 1983, bombing of the U.S. Marine barracks in Beirut. That brought to $8.8 billion the total amount awarded, in eight judgments against Iran, for that bombing, which was perpetrated by elements that formed Lebanese Hezbollah. For more information, see: CRS Report RL31258, *Suits Against Terrorist States by Victims of Terrorism*, by Jennifer K. Elsea.

Executive Order 13599 Impounding Iran-Owned Assets

Several Executive Orders direct the blocking of assets of Iranian entities designated under these Orders. These Orders include E.O. 13224, 13382, 13599, and others as discussed throughout this report. Executive Order 13599, issued February 5, 2012, imposes sanctions on the Central Bank and on other entities determined to be owned or controlled by the Iranian government ("government of Iran"). The order requires that any U.S.-based assets of the Central Bank of Iran, or of any Iranian government-controlled entity, be impounded by U.S. financial institutions. U.S. persons are prohibited from any dealings with such entities. U.S. financial institutions previously were required to merely refuse such transactions with the Central Bank, or return funds to it. Several designations have been made under order, as shown in **Table 5**; on June 21, 2013, OFAC published the names of 38 entities, mostly including oil, petrochemical, and investment companies, determined to meet the definition of "government of Iran."[3] Executive Orders 13224

---

[2] http://www.treasury.gov/resource-center/sanctions/Documents/tar2010.pdf.

[3] http://global.factiva.com/hp/printsavews.aspx?pp=Print&hc=Publication.

and 13382 are discussed later in this report because they block assets of persons involved in support of terrorism or proliferation, respectively. The JPA does not commit the United States to take any action on these or other U.S.-Iran assets disputes.

Sanctions Against Iran's Support for International Terrorism and Regional Activities

The United States began imposing sanctions again Iran again in the mid-1980s. The Secretary of State designated Iran a "state sponsor of terrorism" on January 23, 1984, following the October 1983 bombing of the U.S. Marine barracks in Lebanon perpetrated by elements that later became Hezbollah. This designation triggers substantial sanctions on any nation so designated.

Sanctions Triggered by Terrorism List Designation: Ban on U.S. Aid, Arms Sales, Dual-Use Exports, and Certain Programs for Iran

The U.S. naming of Iran as a "state sponsor of terrorism," commonly referred to as Iran's placement on the U.S. "terrorism list," triggers several sanctions. Terrorism list designations are made under the authority of Section 6(j) of the Export Administration Act of 1979 (P.L. 96-72, as amended), sanctioning countries determined to have provided repeated support for acts of international terrorism. The sanctions triggered by Iran's state sponsor of terrorism designation are:

- *Restrictions on sales of U.S. dual use items.* The restriction is required by the Export Administration Act, as continued through presidential authorities under the International Emergency Economic Powers Act, IEEPA, as implemented by executive orders).

- *Ban on direct U.S. financial assistance and arms sales to Iran.* Section 620A of the Foreign Assistance Act, FAA (P.L. 87-95) and Section 40 of the Arms Export Control Act (P.L. 95-92, as amended), respectively, bar these benefits to terrorism list countries. In addition, successive foreign aid appropriations laws since the late 1980s have banned direct assistance to Iran (loans, credits, insurance, Ex-Im Bank credits) without providing for a waiver.

- *Requirement that the United States vote to oppose multilateral lending.* U.S. representatives are required to vote against multilateral lending to any terrorism list country by Section 1621 of the International Financial Institutions Act (P.L. 95-118, as amended), which was added by Section 327 of the Anti-Terrorism and Effective Death Penalty Act of 1996 (P.L. 104-132). Waivers are provided under these laws.

- *Withholding of U.S. foreign assistance to Suppliers of Terrorism List Countries.* Under Section 620G and 620H of the Foreign Assistance Act, as added by the Anti-Terrorism and Effective Death Penalty Act (sections 325 and 326 of P.L. 104-132), the President is required to withhold foreign aid from any country that provides to a terrorism list country financial assistance or arms. Waivers are provided. Section 321 of that act also makes it a criminal offense for U.S. persons to conduct financial transactions with terrorism list governments.

- *Withholding of U.S. Aid to Organizations that Assist Iran.* Aside from the terrorism list designation, Section 307 of the FAA (added in 1985) names Iran as unable to benefit from U.S. contributions to international organizations, and require proportionate cuts if these institutions work in Iran. For example, if an international organization spends 3% of its budget for programs in Iran, then the United States is required to withhold 3% of its contribution to that international organization. No waiver is provided for.

No Ban on U.S. Humanitarian Aid

The terrorism list designation, and other U.S. sanctions laws, do not bar disaster aid. The United States donated $125,000, through relief agencies, to help victims of two earthquakes in Iran (February and May 1997); $350,000 worth of aid to the victims of a June 22, 2002, earthquake; and $5.7 million in assistance (out of total governmental pledges of about $32 million) for the victims of the December 2003 earthquake in Bam, Iran, which killed as many as 40,000 people. The U.S. military flew in 68,000 kilograms of supplies to Bam.

Removal From Terrorism List/Sanctions Termination

Terminating the sanctions triggered by Iran's terrorism list designation would require Iran's removal from the terrorism list. The Arms Export Control Act spells out two different requirements for a President to remove a country from the list, depending on whether the country's regime has changed.

If the regime has changed, the President can remove a country from the list immediately by certifying that change in a report to Congress.

If the country's regime has not changed, the President must report to Congress 45 days in advance of the effective date of removal. The President must certify that (1) the country has not supported international terrorism within the preceding six months, and (2) the country has provided assurances it will not do so in the future. In this latter circumstance, Congress has the opportunity to block the removal by enacting a joint resolution to that effect. The President has the option of vetoing the joint resolution, in which case blocking the removal would require a congressional veto override vote.

There is no requirement that Iran be removed from the terrorism list as a consequence of the JPA.

Executive Order 13224: Sanctioning Terrorism Supporting Entities

In signing Executive Order 13324 (September 23, 2001), the President ordered the freezing of the U.S.-based assets of and a ban on U.S. transactions with entities determined to be supporting international terrorism. This order was issued two weeks after the September 11, 2001, attacks on the United States, under the authority of the IEEPA, the National Emergencies Act, the U.N. Participation Act of 1945, and Section 301 of the U.S. Code, and initially targeted Al Qaeda-related entities. The Order is therefore not specific to Iran.

Implementation: Iran-related entities designated under the order for terrorism-related activities are listed in the table at the end of this report.

Sanctioning Iranian Involvement in the Region

Some sanctions have been imposed to try to curtail Iran's influence in the region:

- *Executive Order 13438.* On July 7, 2007, President Bush issued Executive Order 13438. The Order sanctions Iranian persons who are posing a threat to Iraqi

---

stability, presumably by providing arms or funds to Shiite militias there. As shown in the tables at the end of this report, some persons sanctioned under the order have been Qods Force officers, some have been Iraqi Shiite militia-linked figures, and some entities have been sanctioned as well.

- *Executive Order 13572.* Issued on April 29, 2011, the Order targets those responsible for human rights abuses and repression of the Syrian people. The Qods Force and a number of Iranian Qods Force officers, including its overall commander Qasem Soleimani, have been sanctioned under this and related Orders, as shown in the tables at the end of the report.

Ban on U.S. Trade and Investment with Iran

The next major sanction imposed on Iran after those required by the terrorism list designation was a ban on U.S. trade with and investment in Iran. It was imposed on May 6, 1995, by President Clinton, through Executive Order 12959, under the authority primarily of the International Emergency Economic Powers Act (IEEPA, 50 U.S.C. 1701 et seq.).[4] IEEPA gives the President wide powers to regulate commerce with a foreign country when a state of emergency is declared in relations with that country. Executive Order 12959 followed and superseded an earlier (March 15, 1995) Executive Order (12957) barring U.S. investment in Iran's energy sector, which accompanied President Clinton's declaration that a "state of emergency" exists with respect to Iran. A subsequent Executive Order, 13059 (August 19, 1997), added a prohibition on U.S. companies' knowingly exporting goods to a third country for incorporation into products destined for Iran. Each March since 1995, the U.S. Administration has renewed a declaration of a state of emergency that triggers the President's trade regulation authority under IEEPA. The operation of the trade regulations is stipulated in Section 560 of the Code of Federal Regulations (Iranian Transactions Regulations, ITRs). *The U.S. trade and investment ban is unaffected by the JPA—with selected exceptions, U.S. firms remain generally banned from the Iran market.*

Codification of the Trade and Investment Ban and U.S.-Iran Trade Figures. Section 103 of the Comprehensive Iran Sanctions, Accountability, and Divestment Act of 2010 (CISADA, P.L. 111-195) codified the ban on U.S trade with Iran. In so doing, it reinstated the full ban on imports that had been relaxed by executive order in April 2000 to allow U.S. importation of Iranian nuts, fruit products (such as pomegranate juice), carpets, and caviar. The relaxations to the trade ban from then until CISADA's effective date of September 29, 2010, account for the fact that U.S. trade with Iran expanded during that period. The restoration of the full import ban explains why U.S. imports from Iran since that time have been negligible (a total of about $2.2 million for all of 2013). U.S. imports from Iran consist primarily of artwork for exhibitions around the United States (and count as imports even though the works return to Iran after the exhibitions conclude). For all of 2013, U.S. exporters sold about $293 million in goods to Iran, mostly grain sales. CISADA also specified exemptions to the ban, such as on exports not only of food and medical goods, but also information technology to support personal communications among the Iranian people, goods to allow civilian aircraft to fly safely, and goods for supporting democracy in Iran.

---

[4] The executive order was issued not only under the authority of IEEPA but also: the National Emergencies Act (50 U.S.C. 1601 et seq.; §505 of the International Security and Development Cooperation Act of 1985 (22 U.S.C. 2349aa-9) and §301 of Title 3, *United States Code.*

Section 101 of the Iran Freedom Support Act (P.L. 109-293) separately codified the ban on U.S. investment in Iran. Section 101 of that law gives the President the authority to terminate sanctions under the Iran Freedom Support Act if he notifies Congress 15 days in advance (or 3 days in advance if there are "exigent circumstances").

Major Provisions: What U.S.-Iran Trade Is Allowed or Prohibited?

The following provisions apply to the U.S. trade ban on Iran as specified in regulations ("Iran Transaction Regulations," ITRs) written pursuant to the various executive orders and laws discussed above. The regulations are administered by the Office of Foreign Assets Control (OFAC) of the Treasury Department.

- *Oil Dealings.* The 1995 trade ban greatly expanded a 1987 ban on imports from Iran under Executive Order 12613 (October 29, 1987). That 1987 ban was imposed under authorities provided in Section 505 of the International Security and Development Cooperation Act of 1985 (22 U.S.C. 2349aa-9). The import ban barred U.S. oil companies from importing Iranian oil but did not ban them from buying Iranian oil and trading it overseas. The 1995 ban prohibits such trading of Iranian oil overseas. The 1995 trade ban does allow U.S. companies to apply for licenses to conduct "swaps" of Caspian Sea oil with Iran. However, these swaps have been prohibited in practice; a Mobil Corporation application to do so was denied in April 1999, and no known applications have been submitted since.

- *The regulations pursuant to the U.S. trade ban do not ban the importation, from foreign refiners, of gasoline or other energy products in which Iranian oil is contained and mixed with oil from other producers.* The product of a refinery is considered a product of the country where that refinery is located, and not a product of Iran, even if the refined product has some Iran-origin crude oil. Much of the Iranian oil that is mixed and imported into the United States was imported from EU countries, such as the Netherlands, which has major refineries in Rotterdam, in particular. However, the EU ban on purchases of Iranian oil has largely mooted this issue, since no EU refineries have imported Iranian oil since July 1, 2012. Only a few other refineries worldwide both continue to receive Iranian oil and export gasoline to the United States, and U.S. gasoline imports from those refineries are minor. Some experts say that it would be feasible to exclude Iranian content from any refinery, if there were a decision to ban U.S. imports of products with any Iranian content.

- *Transshipment and Brokering.* The regulations that implement the trade ban prohibit transshipment of goods across Iran. They also ban any activities by U.S. persons to broker commercial transactions involving Iran.

- *Civilian Airline Parts.* Goods related to the safe operation of civilian aircraft may, on a case-by-case basis, be licensed for export to Iran (§560.528 of Title 31, C.F.R.). In 2006, in the interests of safe operations of civilian aircraft, a sale by General Electric of Airbus engine spare parts to be installed on several Iran Air passenger aircraft (by European airline contractors) was licensed. The Obama Administration licensed the sale to Iran of data to repair certain GE engines for its legacy American-made aircraft in March 16, 2011. However, on June 23, 2011, the Administration sanctioned Iran Air under Executive Order 13382 (see below), rendering future licensing of parts or repairs for Iran Air unclear. Other

Iranian airlines are sanctioned under that and Executive Order 13224 discussed below. The JPA provides for provision of spare civilian airline parts to Iran, specifically including Iran Air (notwithstanding its designation), and relevant provisions of E.O. 13382 have been suspended to enable Iran Air to benefit from this commitment during the JPA period. Boeing and GE have received export licenses to sell aircraft equipment to Iran during the JPA period.[5]

- *Personal Communications, Remittances, and Publishing.* The restrictions do not apply to personal communications (phone calls, e-mails) or to personal remittances—although U.S. banks may process remittances to family members in Iran as long as the remittance is routed through a third country bank and the receiving Iranian bank is not under U.S. sanctions. In December 2004, the trade regulations were modified to allow Americans to engage in ordinary publishing activities with entities in Iran (and Cuba and Sudan). On May 30, 2013, OFAC issued a general license for the exportation to Iran of goods (such as cellphones) and services, on a fee basis, that enhance the ability of the Iranian people to access communication technology.

- *Food and Medical Exports.* Since April 1999, commercial sales of food and medical products to Iran have been allowed, on a case-by-case basis and subject to OFAC licensing. Among earlier relaxations, on October 22, 2012, OFAC attempted to facilitate medical sales by issuing a list of medical products, such as scalpels, prosthetics, canes, burn dressings, and other products that could be sold to Iran under "general license"—no export license requirement. That list was updated on July 25, 2013, to include electrocardiogram, electroencephalogram, and dialysis machines and other medical products. According to OFAC, licenses for exports of medical products not on the list are routinely expedited for sale to Iran, and the U.S. government has been informing foreign banks that financing such transactions is not sanctionable. The JPA commits the United States and its partners to facilitate humanitarian sales to Iran. Implementing that commitment did not require modifications to U.S. trade regulations on that issue.

- OFAC regulations have a specific definition of "food" that can be licensed for sale to Iran, and that definition excludes alcohol, cigarettes, gum, or fertilizer.[6] This definition addresses information in a December 24, 2010[7] article that said that OFAC had approved exports to Iran of such condiments as ice cream sprinkles, chewing gum, food additives, hot sauces, body-building supplements, and other goods that have uses other than purely nutritive. Some of the licensed U.S. goods were sold through a Revolutionary Guard-owned chain of stores in Iran called Qods, as well as a government-owned Shahrvand store.

- *Humanitarian and Related Services.* Private non-financial donations by U.S. residents to Iranian victims of natural disasters (such as mailed packages of food, toys, clothes, etc.) are not prohibited, but donations to relief organizations require a specific OFAC license, because such transfers generally require use of the

---

[5] Reuters, February 21, 2014; Exclusive: Boeing Says Gets U.S. License to Sell Spare Parts to Iran. Reuters, April 4, 2014.

[6] http://www.treasury.gov/resource-center/sanctions/Programs/Documents/gl_food_exports.pdf.

[7] The information in this bullet is taken from: Jo Becker, "With U.S. Leave, Companies Skirt Iran Sanctions," *New York Times*, December 24, 2010.

international banking system. Prior to September 2013, all NGOs that sought to perform relief efforts in Iran required a specific license to do so, which apparently made work in Iran impractical. On September 10, 2013, the Treasury Department eliminated licensing requirements for the provision to Iran of services for health projects, disaster relief, wildlife conservation, human rights projects, and activities related to sports matches and events. The amended regulation also allows importation from Iran of services related to sporting activities, including sponsorship of players, coaching, referees, and training. In some cases, such as the earthquake in Bam in 2003 and the earthquake in northwestern Iran in August 2012, OFAC has issued blanket temporary general licensing for relief organizations to perform relief efforts in Iran. The licensing requirements in the latter case allowed an NGO to transfer up to $300,000 without requiring a specific license.

- *Export Financing.* As far as financing of approved U.S. sales to Iran, private letters of credit (from non-Iranian banks) can be used to finance approved transactions. Title IX of the Trade Sanctions Reform and Export Enhancement Act of 2000 (P.L. 106-387)[8] bans the use of official credit guarantees for food and medical sales to Iran and other countries on the U.S. terrorism list, except Cuba, although allowing for a presidential waiver to permit such credit guarantees. No U.S. Administration has authorized credit guarantees, to date. It is not clear whether a waiver will be provided for such financing as a consequence of the November 24, 2013, interim nuclear deal with Iran.

Application to Foreign Subsidiaries of U.S. Firms

The U.S. trade ban does not bar subsidiaries of U.S. firms from dealing with Iran, as long as the subsidiary has no operational relationship to—or control by—the parent company. For legal and policy purposes, foreign subsidiaries are considered foreign persons, not U.S. persons, and are subject to the laws of the country in which the subsidiaries are incorporated. Section 218 of the Iran Threat Reduction and Syrian Human Rights Act (P.L. 112-158) applies the U.S. trade ban to foreign subsidiaries if (1) the subsidiary is more than 50% owned by the U.S. parent; (2) the parent firm holds a majority on the Board of Directors; or (3) the parent firm directs the operations of the subsidiary. However, many subsidiaries operate entirely autonomously and might not meet the criteria for sanctionability stipulated in that law.

---

[8] The title is called the "Trade Sanctions Reform and Export Enhancement Act of 2000."

Trade Ban Easing and Termination

The trade ban has been codified by CISADA, as noted.

Termination:

Section 401 of CISADA provides for the President to terminate the trade ban codification provision of CISADA (Section 103). The provision can be terminated if the Administration certifies to Congress that Iran has no longer satisfies the requirements to be designated as a state sponsor of terrorism and that Iran has ceased pursuing *and* dismantled its nuclear, biological, and chemical weapons and ballistic missiles and related launch technology.

Alternatively, the trade ban provision in CISADA could be repealed outright by congressional action.

Waiver Authority

In addition, Section 103(b)(vi) of CISADA allows the President to license exports to Iran if he determines that doing so is in the national interest of the United States. This gives the President flexibility to ease the ban on U.S. exports through executive action. There is no similar provision in CISADA to ease the ban on U.S. imports from Iran through a national interest determination.

There are no indications that the ban on U.S. trade with or investment in Iran is required under the November 24, 2013, interim nuclear deal, although some transactions might be authorized as a consequence, as discussed above. There are no indications Iran will demand the U.S. trade and investment ban be lifted or no longer implemented as part of a comprehensive nuclear deal.

Energy and Other Sector Sanctions: Iran Sanctions Act (ISA) and Related Laws and Executive Orders

Since 1996, Congress and successive Administrations have put in place steps to try to force foreign firms to choose between participating in the U.S. market and continuing to conduct various energy-related transactions with Iran. The intent of energy sanctions has been to put pressure on Iran's economy and its leadership calculations, and to deny Iran the financial resources to further its nuclear and WMD programs and support terrorist organizations. Iran's petroleum sector is vital to the Iran state and economy—prior to the imposition of oil export-related sanctions in 2012 it generated about 20% of Iran's GDP, about 80% of its foreign exchange earnings, and about 50% of its government revenue.

Iran's oil sector is as old as the petroleum industry itself (early 20th century), and Iran's onshore oil fields are past peak production and in need of substantial investment. Iran has 136.3 billion barrels of proven oil reserves, the third largest after Saudi Arabia and Canada. With the exception of relatively small swap and barter arrangements with neighboring countries, virtually all of Iran's oil exports flow through the Strait of Hormuz, which carries about one-third of all internationally traded oil. Iran's large natural gas resources (940 trillion cubic feet, exceeded only by Russia) were virtually undeveloped when ISA was first enacted. Its small gas exports are mainly to Armenia and Turkey; most of its gas is injected into its oil fields to boost their production.

The Iran Sanctions Act, Amendments, and Related Applications

The Iran Sanctions Act (ISA) has been a key component of U.S. sanctions against Iran's energy sector, and it has been expanded to sanction dealings with other Iranian economic sectors. As initially enacted, ISA sought to thwart Iran's opening of the sector to foreign investment in late 1995. To accommodate its insistence on retaining control of its national resources, Iran used a "buy-back" investment program in which foreign firms gradually recoup their investments as oil and gas is discovered and then produced. In September 1995, Senator Alfonse D'Amato introduced a bill to sanction foreign firms' exports to Iran of energy technology. A revised version instead sanctioning *investment* in Iran's energy sector, and also applying all provisions to Libya passed the Senate. The Iran and Libya Sanctions Act (ILSA) was signed on August 5, 1996 (H.R. 3107, P.L. 104-172). It was later retitled the Iran Sanctions Act after it terminated with respect to Libya in 2006.

ISA was the first major "extra-territorial sanction" on Iran—a sanction that authorizes U.S. penalties against third country firms. ISA's application has been further expanded by several laws enacted since 2010 that amend its provisions.

Key "Triggers"

ISA consists of a number of "triggers"—transactions with Iran that would be considered violations of ISA and could cause a firm or entity to be sanctioned under ISA's provisions. When triggered, ISA provides for a number of different sanctions that could harm a foreign firm's business opportunities in the United States.

"Investment" To Develop Iran's Oil and Gas Fields

ISA requires the President to sanction companies (entities, persons) that make an "investment"[9] of more than $20 million[10] in one year in Iran's energy sector.[11] The definition of "investment" in ISA (§14 (9)) includes not only equity and royalty arrangements but any contract that includes "responsibility for the development of petroleum resources" of Iran. The definition includes additions to existing investment (added by P.L. 107-24) and pipelines to or through Iran and contracts to lead the construction, upgrading, or expansions of energy projects (added by the Comprehensive Iran Sanctions, Accountability, and Divestment Act of 2010 [CISADA; P.L. 111-195]).

Implementation: Several firms have been sanctioned under ISA for investing in Iran's oil and gas fields, as discussed below.

Sales of Weapons Related Technology and Uranium Mining Ventures

The Iran Freedom Support Act (P.L. 109-293, signed September 30, 2006) amended ISA by adding Section 5(b)(1) subjecting to ISA sanctions firms or persons determined to have sold to Iran (1) technology useful for weapons of mass destruction (WMD) or (2) "destabilizing numbers

---

[9] As amended by CISADA (P.L. 111-195), these definitions include pipelines to or through Iran, as well as contracts to lead the construction, upgrading, or expansions of energy projects. CISADA also changes the definition of investment to eliminate the exemption from sanctions for sales of energy-related equipment to Iran, if such sales are structured as investments or ongoing profit-earning ventures.

[10] Under §4(d) of the original act, for Iran, the threshold dropped to $20 million, from $40 million, one year after enactment, when U.S. allies did not join a multilateral sanctions regime against Iran. However, P.L. 111-195 explicitly sets the threshold investment level at $20 million. For Libya, the threshold was $40 million, and sanctionable activity included export to Libya of technology banned by Pan Am 103-related Security Council Resolutions 748 (March 31, 1992) and 883 (November 11, 1993).

[11] The original ISA definition of energy sector included oil and natural gas, and CISADA added to that definition: liquefied natural gas (LNG), oil or LNG tankers, and products to make or transport pipelines that transport oil or LNG.

---

and types" of advanced conventional weapons. (Sanctions apply if the exporter knew or had cause to know that the final destination of the items sold would be Iran.)

Entities determined by the Administration to participate in a joint venture with Iran relating to the mining, production, or transportation of uranium are sanctionable under ISA. Under *Section 5(b)(2)* added by the Iran Threat Reduction and Syria Human Rights Act (P.L. 112-158, signed August 10, 2012).

Implementation: No ISA sanctions have been imposed on any entities under these provisions.

Sales of Gasoline and Related Equipment and Services

Section 102(a) of the Comprehensive Iran Sanctions, Accountability, and Divestment Act of 2010 (CISADA, signed on July 1, 2010, P.L. 111-195) amended Section 5 of ISA to exploit Iran's dependency on imported gasoline (40% dependency at that time). It followed legislation such as H.R. 2880 (110th Congress, not enacted); P.L. 111-85 that prohibited the use of U.S. funds to fill the Strategic Petroleum Reserve with products from firms that sell gasoline to Iran; and P.L. 111-117 that denied Ex-Im Bank credits to any firm that sold gasoline or related equipment and services to Iran—initiatives that prompted Reliance Industries Ltd. of India to cease new sales of gasoline to Iran as of December 2008. (The Ex-Im Bank, in August 2008, had extended $900 million in financing guarantees to Relianced.) The provision made sanctionable:

- sales to Iran of over $1 million worth (or $5 million in a one year period) of gasoline and related aviation and other fuels. (Fuel oil, a petroleum by-product, is not included in the definition of refined petroleum.)

- sales to Iran of equipment or services (same dollar threshold as above) which would help Iran make or import gasoline. Examples of such sales include equipment and services that Iran can use to construct or maintain its oil refineries, or provision of related services such as shipping or port operations.

Implementation: Several firms, as discussed below, have been sanctioned under ISA for selling or shipping gasoline to Iran.

Sales of Energy Sector Equipment, Services, and Petrochemicals

An Executive Order, 13590 (November 21, 2011), was codified by Section 201 of the Iran Threat Reduction and Syria Human Rights Act of 2012 (ITRSHA, P.L. 112-158). The ITRSHA provision added Section 5(a)(5 and 6) to ISA sanctioning firms that:

- provide to Iran $1 million or more (or $5 million in a one year period) worth of goods or services that Iran could use to maintain or enhance its oil and gas sector. This made sanctionable, for example, transactions with Iran by global oil services firms and the sale to Iran of energy industry gear such as drills, pumps, vacuums, oil rigs, and the like.

- provide to Iran $250,000 (or $1 million in a one year period) worth of goods or services that Iran could use to maintain or expand its production of petrochemical products.[12] *This provision was not required to be waived as a consequence of the November 24, 2013, interim nuclear deal with Iran, and was not waived.*

Implementation: No firms have been sanctioned under these provisions.

Purchasing of Iranian Crude Oil and Petrochemical Products

Executive Order 13622 (July 30, 2012) applies virtually all of the same sanctions as ISA—as well as restrictions on foreign banks (see below)—to entities that the Administration determines have:

- purchased oil or other petroleum products from Iran.[13] *The part of this provision pertaining to petrochemical purchases will need to be waived as a consequence of the interim nuclear deal.*

- conducted transactions with the National Iranian Oil Company (NIOC) or Naftiran Intertrade Company (NICO).

Under the Order, sanctions do not apply if the parent country of the entity has received an exemption under Section 1245 of P.L. 112-81—an exemption earned for "significantly reducing" oil purchases from Iran. (See below for more information on the exemption process.) *A law cannot be amended by executive order and E.O. 13622 does not amend ISA.*

Implementation: Several firms were sanctioned under this order on May 31, 2013, for petrochemical sales to Iran.

Sanctions on transactions related to purchasing Iranian crude oil were codified by Section 201 of the Iran Threat Reduction and Syria Human Rights Act (P.L. 112-158, signed August 10, 2012). It amends ISA by applying ISA sanctions to entities determined by the Administration to have:

- Owned a vessel that was used to transport Iranian crude oil. This sanction does not apply in cases of transporting oil to countries that have received exemptions under P.L. 112-81, discussed below. The section also *authorizes but does not require* the President, subject to regulations, to prohibit a ship from putting to port in the United States for two years, if it is owned by a person sanctioned under this provision. *(Adds Section 5(a)(7) to ISA.)*

- Participated in a joint oil and gas development venture with Iran, outside Iran, if that venture was established after January 1, 2002. The effective date exempts energy ventures in the Caspian Sea, such as the Shah Deniz oil field there. *(Adds Section 5(a)(4 to ISA).)*

Implementation. Some firms, as shown below, have been sanctioned for providing vessels for the shipment of crude oil to Iran.

---

[12] A definition of chemicals and products considered "petrochemical products" is found in a Policy Guidance statement. See, *Federal Register*, November 13, 2012, http://www.regulations.gov/#!documentDetail;D=DOS_FRDOC_0001-2175.

[13] A definition of what chemicals and products are considered "petroleum products" for the purposes of the order are in the policy guidance issued November 13, 2012, http://www.regulations.gov/#!documentDetail;D=DOS_FRDOC_0001-2175.

Insurance for Iranian Oil Entities and Purchases of Iranian Bonds

Separate provisions of the Iran Threat Reduction and Syria Human Rights Act (Sections 212, 213, and 302) *do not specifically amend ISA*, but require the application of 5 out of 12 ISA sanctions on any company:

- that provides insurance or re-insurance for the National Iranian Oil Company (NIOC) or the National Iranian Tanker Company (NITC); or

- that purchases or facilitates the issuance of sovereign debt of the government of Iran, including Iranian government bonds.

Dealings with Iran's Energy, Shipbuilding, and Shipping Sector

The National Defense Authorization Act for FY2013 (H.R. 4310, P.L. 112-239, signed January 2, 2013) Subtitle D, "The Iran Freedom and Counter-Proliferation Act" (IFCA), *does not amend ISA* but imposes at least 5 out the 12 ISA sanctions (as of July 1, 2013, 180 days after enactment) on entities determined to have:

- provided goods or services to the energy, shipbuilding, and shipping sectors of Iran, or to port operations there—or which provide insurance for such transactions. This is under Section 1244 of IFCA, which also blocks U.S.-based property and U.S.-based banking activity on violators. *The sanctions do not apply when such transactions involve purchases of Iranian oil by countries that have active exemptions under P.L. 112-81 or to the purchase of natural gas from Iran (or most transactions related to such gas purchases).*

- provided underwriting services, insurance, or reinsurance for a broad range of transactions with Iran, including those related to shipping oil, gasoline, or other goods for the energy, shipping, or shipbuilding sectors in Iran. This is under Section 1246 of IFCA. *There is no exception to this sanction for countries exempted under P.L. 112-81.*

- Section 1248 of IFCA sanctions Iran's state broadcasting establishment (Islamic Republic of Iran Broadcasting) as a human rights abuser, triggering sanctions under Section 105 of CISADA.

- *Dealings in Precious Metals.* Section 1245 of IFCA imposes at least 5 out of 12 ISA sanctions on entities that provide precious metals to Iran (including gold) or semi-finished metals or software for integrating industrial processes. The section therefore affects foreign firms that transfer gold or other precious metals to Iran in exchange for oil or any other product. *There is no exception to this sanction for countries exempted under P.L. 112-81. The provision does not amend ISA.* This essentially codifies Section 5 of Executive Order 13622 that blocks U.S.-based property of individuals or firms determined to have helped Iran purchase U.S. bank notes or precious metals or to have provided financial support to NIOC, NICO, or the Central Bank of Iran. Executive Order 13645 of June 3, 2013, (Section 16), applies the restriction to transfers of stones or jewels.

Waiver authority is discussed in the box on ISA waivers below.

The Automotive Sector and Rial Trading

Executive Order 13645 of June 3, 2013, (effective July 1, 2013):

- imposes ISA sanctions on firms that supply goods or services to Iran's automotive (cars, trucks, buses, motorcycles, and related parts) sector, and blocks foreign banks from the U.S. market if they finance transactions with Iran's automotive sector. (An executive order cannot amend a law, so the order does not amend ISA.) *This provision was suspended to implement the November 24, 2013, interim nuclear deal with Iran.*

- blocks U.S.-based property and prohibits U.S. bank accounts for foreign banks that conduct transactions in Iran's currency, the rial, or hold rial accounts. This provision most likely will affect banks in countries bordering or nearby Iran that sometimes have dealt in the rial.

- blocks U.S.-based property of any person that conducts transactions with any Iranian entity on the list of Specially Designated Nationals (SDNs) or Blocked Persons.

Mandate and Time Frame to Investigate ISA Violations

In the original version of ISA, there was no firm requirement, and no time limit, for the Administration to investigate potential violations and determine that a firm has violated ISA's provisions. CISADA, Section 102(g)(5), altered that by mandating that the Administration begin an investigation of potential ISA violations when there is "credible information" about a potential violation. The same section made mandatory the 180-day time limit for a determination of violation. Under Section 102(h)(5), the mandate to investigate gasoline related sales can be delayed an additional 180 days if an Administration report, submitted to Congress by June 1, 2011, asserts that its policies have produced a significant result in sales of gasoline to Iran. (No such report was submitted.) Earlier, P.L. 109-293, the "Iran Freedom Support Act" (signed September 30, 2006) amended ISA by calling for, *but not requiring*, a 180-day time limit for a violation determination (there is no time limit in the original law).[14]

A subsequent law, the Iran Threat Reduction and Syria Human Rights Act (P.L. 112-158), contains a provision to define "credible information" to begin an investigation of a violation. The law defines credible information to include a corporate announcement or corporate filing to its shareholders that it has undertaken transactions with Iran that are potentially sanctionable under ISA. It also says the President *may* (not mandatory) use as credible information reports from the Government Accountability Office and the Congressional Research Service.

Oversight Mechanisms: Reports Required

The Iran Threat Reduction and Syria Human Rights Act (P.L. 112-158) sets up several mechanisms for Congress to oversee whether the Administration is investigating ISA violations. Section 223 requires a Government Accountability Office report, within 120 days of enactment,

---

[14] Other ISA amendments under that law included recommending against U.S. nuclear agreements with countries that supply nuclear technology to Iran and expanding provisions of the USA Patriot Act (P.L. 107-56) to curb money-laundering for use to further WMD programs.

and another such report a year later, on companies that have undertaken specified activities with Iran that might constitute violations of ISA. Section 224 amends a reporting requirement in Section 110(b) of CISADA by requiring an Administration report every 180 days on investment in Iran's energy sector, joint ventures with Iran, and estimates of Iran's imports and exports of petroleum products. The GAO reports have been issued; there is no information available on whether the required Administration reports have been issued as well.

Available Sanctions Under ISA

Once a firm is determined to be a violator, the original version of ISA required the imposition of *two* of a menu of six sanctions on that firm. CISADA added three new possible sanctions and required the imposition of at least three out of the nine against violators. CISADA amended ISA by adding three available sanctions and requiring imposition on *5 out of the 12* available sanctions. Executive Order 13590, and the July 30, 2012, executive order, discussed above, provide for exactly the same penalties as those in ISA. The 12 available sanctions against the sanctioned entity, from which the Secretary of State or the Treasury can select, are:

1. denial of Export-Import Bank loans, credits, or credit guarantees for U.S. exports to the sanctioned entity (original ISA)

2. denial of licenses for the U.S. export of military or militarily useful technology to the entity (original ISA)

3. denial of U.S. bank loans exceeding $10 million in one year to the entity (original ISA)

4. if the entity is a financial institution, a prohibition on its service as a primary dealer in U.S. government bonds; and/or a prohibition on its serving as a repository for U.S. government funds (each counts as one sanction) (original ISA)

5. prohibition on U.S. government procurement from the entity (original ISA)

6. prohibitions in transactions in foreign exchange by the entity (added by CISADA)

7. prohibition on any credit or payments between the entity and any U.S. financial institution (added by CISADA)

8. prohibition of the sanctioned entity from acquiring, holding, using, or trading any U.S.-based property which the sanctioned entity has a (financial) interest in (added by CISADA)

9. restriction on imports from the sanctioned entity, in accordance with the International Emergency Economic Powers Act (IEEPA; 50 U.S.C. 1701) (original ISA)

10. a ban on a U.S. person from investing in or purchasing significant amounts of equity or debt instruments of a sanctioned person (added by Iran Threat Reduction and Syria Human Rights Act, P.L. 112-158)

11. exclusion from the United States of corporate officers or controlling shareholders of a sanctioned firm (added by P.L. 112-158)

12. imposition of any of the ISA sanctions on principal offices of a sanctioned firm (added by P.L. 112-158).

Mandatory Sanction: Prohibition on Contracts with the U.S. Government

There is an additional *mandatory* sanction under ISA. CISADA (§102(b)) added a requirement in ISA that companies, as a condition of obtaining a U.S. government contract, certify to the relevant U.S. government agency that the firm—*and any companies it owns or controls*—are not violating ISA. Regulations to implement this requirement were issued on September 29, 2010.

ISA Waiver, Exemptions, and Sunset Provisions

ISA Waiver Provisions

The President has the authority to waive sanctions on firms determined to have violated ISA provisions. Under the original version of ISA to waive sanctions if he certifies that doing so is *important* to the U.S. national interest (§9(c)). CISADA (§102(c)) changed the 9(c) ISA waiver standard to "*necessary*" to the national interest, and the Iran Threat Reduction Act modified the standard further to "*essential to the national security interests*" of the United States. For sanctionable transactions involving WMD equipment, the waiver standard, as modified by the Iran Threat Reduction Act, is "'*vital to the national security interests of the United States.*"

Under the original version of ISA, there was also waiver authority (§4(c)) if the parent country of the violating firm joined a sanctions regime against Iran. This waiver provision was changed by the Iran Freedom Support Act (P.L. 109-293) to allow for a waiver determination based on U.S. vital national security interests. The Section 4(c) waiver was altered again, by CISADA, to provide for a six month (renewable) waiver if doing so is "*vital to the national interest,*" *and* if the parent country of the violating entity is "closely cooperating" with U.S. efforts against Iran's WMD and advanced conventional weapons program. The criterion of "closely cooperating" is defined in the conference report as implementing all U.N. sanctions against Iran. It could be argued that using a Section 4 waiver, rather than a Section 9 waiver, would support U.S. diplomacy with the parent country of the offending entity.

ISA (§5(f)) also contains several exceptions such that the President is not required to impose sanctions that prevent procurement of defense articles and services under existing contracts, in cases where a firm is the sole source supplier of a particular defense article or service. The President also is not required to prevent procurement of essential spare parts or component parts.

Related IFCA Waiver Authority

Sections 1244 and 1245 of IFCA provide for a waiver of sanctions for 180 days, renewable for 180 day periods, if such a waiver is determined to be vital to U.S. national security. These sections were waived in order to implement the JPA. In addition, Section 5(a)(7) of ISA was waived to allow for certain transactions with NIOC and NITC.

"Special Rule" Exempting Firms That End Their Business with Iran

Under a provision added by CISADA (§102(g)(5)), ISA provides a means—a so-called "special rule"—for firms to avoid ISA sanctions by pledging to verifiably end their business with Iran and to forgo any sanctionable business with Iran in the future. Under the special rule, the Administration is not required to make a determination of sanctionability against a firm that makes such pledges. The special rule has been invoked on several occasions, as discussed below. However, there is some imprecision in the time frame under which countries can wind down their Iran business, and some firms could work in Iran for several more years under their pledges. Energy firms insist they needed time to wind down their investments in Iran because, under the buy-back program used by Iran, the energy firms are paid back their investment over time, making it highly costly for them to suddenly end operations in Iran.

Termination Process and Requirements

In its entirety, ISA application to Iran would terminate if the Administration certifies that three requirements are met: (1) that Iran has ceased its efforts to acquire WMD; (2) that Iran has been removed from the U.S. list of state sponsors of terrorism; *and* (3) that Iran no longer "poses a significant threat" to U.S. national security and U.S. allies.[15]

This termination provision, and the sunset provision discussed below, *do not apply to those laws that apply ISA sanctions without specifically amending ISA.* The executive orders and laws that apply ISA sanctions to specified violators *but without amending ISA itself* can be revoked by a superseding executive order or congressional action that amends or repeals the provisions involved.

Sunset Provisions

ISA is currently scheduled to sunset on December 31, 2016, as provided for by CISADA. This followed prior sunset extensions to December 31, 2011, (by P.L. 109-293), and to December 31, 2006 (P.L. 107-24, August 3, 2001). The original law provided for a sunset date of August 5, 2001. P.L. 107-24 also required an Administration report on ISA's effectiveness within 24 to 30 months of enactment; that report was submitted to Congress in January 2004 and did not recommend that ISA be repealed.

---

[15] This termination requirement added by P.L. 109-293, which formally removed Libya from the Act. Application of the Act to Libya terminated on April 23, 2004, with a determination that Libya had fulfilled U.N. requirements.

Clarification of Responsibilities: Executive Order 13574

On May 23, 2011, President Obama issued Executive Order 13574 clarifying that it is the responsibility of the Treasury Department to implement those ISA sanctions that involve the financial sector, including bans on loans, credits, and foreign exchange for, or imports from the sanctioned entity, as well as blockage of property of the sanctioned entity (if these sanctions are selected by the Secretary of State, who makes the decision which penalties to impose on sanctioned entities).

Interpretations and Administration of ISA and Related Laws

The sections below analyze how ISA, as amended by related laws, have been interpreted and implemented through real-world cases and examples.

Application to Energy Pipelines

ISA's definition of sanctionable "investment" has been consistently interpreted by successive Administrations to include construction of energy pipelines to or through Iran. Such pipelines are deemed to help Iran develop its petroleum (oil and natural gas) sector. This interpretation was reinforced by amendments to ISA in CISADA, which specifically included in the definition of petroleum resources "products used to construct or maintain pipelines used to transport oil or liquefied natural gas." In March 2012, then-Secretary of State Clinton made clear that the Obama Administration interprets the provision to be applicable from the beginning of pipeline construction, and not from the start of oil or gas flow through a finished project.[16]

Implementation. No gas pipelines built linking Iran to neighboring countries have been sanctioned under ISA. Specific pipeline projects that are under various stages of construction are discussed in the international compliance section below.

Application to Crude Oil Purchases

The original version of ISA did not make sanctionable purchases of oil from Iran. Executive Order 13622 and P.L. 112-158 essentially render purchasing Iranian oil sanctionable—if the parent country of the energy buyer or shipper has not received a sanctions exemption under P.L. 112-81, which is discussed below. Any new customer for Iranian oil is automatically sanctionable under the Order and P.L. 112-81.

Application to Natural Gas Purchases from Iran/Shah Deniz Exception

The FY2013 National Defense Authorization Act (P.L. 112-239) bars dealings with Iran's energy sector broadly—*but specifically excludes from sanctionability purchases of natural gas from Iran.* Still, *payments* for the natural gas might be subject to sanctions as discussed elsewhere in this report. *Purchases* of Iranian gas are distinguishable from the *construction of natural gas pipelines* involving Iran which, as discussed, does constitute potentially sanctionable activity.

---

[16] http://dawn.com/2012/03/01/tough-us-warning-on-iran-gas-pipeline/.

The effective dates of U.S. sanctions laws also excludes long-standing joint natural gas projects that involve some Iranian firms—particularly the Shah Deniz gas project, a natural gas project in the Caspian Sea. The project is run by a consortium in which Iran's Naftiran Intertrade Copmany (NICO) holds a passive 10% share. The other partners in the venture are BP, Azerbaijan's natural gas firm SOCAR, Russia's Lukoil, and other firms. NICO has been sanctioned under ISA, as discussed below. However, an OFAC factsheet updated on November 28, 2012, states that the Shah Deniz consortium, as a whole, is not determined to be "a person owned or controlled by" the government of Iran, as defined in Executive Order 13599. According to the factsheet, transactions with the consortium would not violate U.S. trade regulations on Iran nor require a license from OFAC. That appears to apply to the second phase of the project that is now under way, which involves NICO at the same level of ownership and will carry gas to Europe.

Application to Liquefied Natural Gas Development

The original version of ISA did not apply to the development by Iran of a liquefied natural gas (LNG) export capability. Iran has no LNG export terminals, in part because the technology for such terminals is patented by U.S. firms and unavailable for sale to Iran. However, CISADA specifically includes LNG in the definition of petroleum resources and therefore made LNG investment in Iran—or supply of LNG tankers or pipelines to Iran—sanctionable.

Application to Private Financing but Not Official Credit Guarantee Agencies

The definitions of investment and other sanctionable activity under ISA clearly include financing for investment in Iran's energy sector, or for sales of gasoline and refinery-related equipment and services. Therefore, banks and other financial institutions that assist energy investment and refining and gasoline procurement activities could be sanctioned under ISA.

However, these definitions—including those in Executive Order 13622 and in P.L. 112-158—are not interpreted to apply to official credit guarantee agencies—such as France's COFACE and Germany's Hermes. These credit guarantee agencies are arms of their parent governments, and ISA does not provide for sanctioning governments or their agencies. Early versions of CISADA would have made these entities sanctionable but this was not included in the final law, out of concern for alienating U.S. allies.

Application to Iranian Energy Institutions/NIOC and NITC

As noted above, provisions of P.L. 112-158 and Executive Order 13622—*although they do not amend ISA*—apply ISA sanctions to dealings with the National Iranian Oil Company (NIOC), which is supervised by the Oil Ministry, the National Iranian Tanker Company (NITC), and a previously sanctioned firm, Naftiran Intertrade Company (NICO), which is a subsidiary of NIOC.

Under Section 302 of the Iran Threat Reduction and Syria Human Rights Act (P.L. 112-158), any person who engages in a significant transaction with NIOC and NITC is subject to the imposition of 5 out of 12 ISA sanctions. Section 312 of that law required an Administration determination, within 45 days of enactment (by September 24, 2012) whether NIOC and NITC are IRGC agents or affiliates. If such a determination is made, financial transactions with NIOC and NITC would be sanctionable under CISADA (prohibition on opening U.S.-based accounts).

Implementation. On September 24, 2012, the Department of the Treasury informed Congress that it had determined that NIOC and NITC are agents or affiliates of the IRGC. As noted below, on November 8, 2012, the Treasury Department named NIOC as a proliferation entity under Executive Order 13382. In accordance with Section 104 of CISADA, that designation bars any foreign bank determined to have dealt directly with NIOC (including with a NIOC bank account in a foreign country) from opening a U.S.-based account.

Some major components of NIOC have not been sanctioned, including the Iranian Offshore Oil Company; the National Iranian Gas Export Co.; and Petroleum Engineering and Development Co. There are also independent Iranian energy firms, such as Pasargad Oil Co, Zagros Petrochem Co, Sazeh Consultants, Qeshm Energy, and Sadid Industrial Group. Their relations with NIOC or the Revolutionary Guard (see below) are unclear, and none of these independent firms has been sanctioned under any U.S. law or executive order.

Sanctions on dealings with NIOC and NITC were waived in accordance with the JPA.

Sanctions Imposed Under ISA

The European Union (EU) opposed ISA as an extraterritorial application of U.S. law. In April 1997, the United States and the EU agreed to avoid a trade confrontation over ISA and a separate Cuba sanctions law (P.L. 104-114). The agreement involved the promise by the EU not to file any complaint with the World Trade Organization (WTO) over this issue, in exchange for the eventual May 18, 1998, announcement by the Clinton Administration to waive ISA sanctions ("national interest"—§9c—waiver) on the first project determined to be in violation—a $2 billion[17] contract, signed in September 1997, for Total SA of France and its partners, Gazprom of Russia and Petronas of Malaysia, to develop phases 2 and 3 of the 25+ phase South Pars gas field. The EU, for its part, pledged to increase cooperation with the United States on nonproliferation and counterterrorism. Then-Secretary of State Albright, in the May 18, 1998, waiver announcement, indicated that similar future such projects by EU firms in Iran would not be sanctioned, provided overall EU cooperation against Iranian terrorism and proliferation continued.[18] The EU sanctions against Iran imposed since 2010 have largely rendered this understanding moot because EU firms are barred from investing in Iran's energy sector.

The Obama Administration has used ISA authorities to discourage companies from continuing their business with Iran. This is a contrast from the first 14 years after ISA's passage, in which successive Administrations hesitated to confront companies of partner countries. State Department reports to Congress on ISA, required every six months, do not specifically state which foreign companies, if any, are still being investigated for ISA violations. No publication of such deals has been placed in the *Federal Register,* as required by Section 5e of ISA.

The companies for which ISA determinations have been announced are listed in the table below.

---

[17] Dollar figures for investments in Iran represent public estimates of the amounts investing firms are expected to spend over the life of a project, which might in some cases be several decades.

[18] Text of announcement of waiver decision by then-Secretary of State Madeleine Albright, containing expectation of similar waivers in the future, at http://www.parstimes.com/law/albright_southpars.html.

Table 1. ISA Sanctions Determinations

Date	Companies/Country	Status/Comment
May 18, 1998	Total SA (France); Gazprom (Russia); and Petronas (Malaysia)	Waived. ISA Violation determined but sanctions waived in line with U.S.-EU agreement discussed in text above.
Sept. 30, 2010	Naftiran Intertrade Co. (NICO) Switzerland, Iran	Sanctioned. For activities to develop Iran's energy sector
Sept. 30, 2010	Total (France); Statoil (Norway); ENI (Italy); and Royal Dutch Shell (Britain, Netherlands)	Exempted. Under from sanctions under ISA "special rule" for pledging to wind down work on Iran energy fields.
Nov. 17, 2010	Inpex (Japan)	Exempted. Special rule applied for announcement one month earlier that it divested its remaining 10% stake in Azadegan oil field development.
March 29, 2011	Belarusneft (Belarus, subsidiary of Belneftekhim)	Sanctioned. For $500 million contract with NICO (see above) to develop Jofeir oil field. Other subsidiaries of Belneftekhim were sanctioned in 2007 under E.O. 13405 related to policy on Belarus.
May 24, 2011	Petrochemical Commercial Company International (PCCI) of Bailiwick of Jersey and Iran; Royal Oyster Group (UAE); Tanker Pacific (Singapore); Allvale Maritime (Liberia); Societie Anonyme Monegasque Et Aerienne (SAMAMA, Monaco); Speedy Ship (UAE/Iran); Associated Shipbroking (Monaco); and Petroleos de Venezuela (PDVSA, Venezuela).	Sanctioned. Under CISADA amendment to ISA imposing sanctions for selling gasoline to Iran or helping Iran import gasoline. Allvale Maritime and SAMAMA determinations were issued on September 13, 2011, to "clarify" the May 24 determinations that had named Ofer Brothers Group. The two, as well as Tanker Pacific, are affiliated with a Europe-based trust linked to deceased Ofer brother Sami Ofer, and not Ofer Brothers Group based in Israel. The firms named were subjected primarily to the financial-related sanctions provided in ISA. U.S.-based subsidiaries of PDVSA, such as Citgo, were not sanctioned and U.S. purchases of Venezuelan oil were not affected.
Jan. 12, 2012	Zhuhai Zhenrong Co. (China); Kuo Oil Pte Ltd. (Singapore); FAL Oil Co. (UAE)	Sanctioned. For brokering sales or making sales to Iran of gasoline.
Aug. 12, 2012	Sytrol (Syria)	Sanctioned. For sales of gasoline to Iran.
Mar. 14, 2013	Dr. Dimitris Cambis; Impire Shipping; Kish Protection and Indemnity (Iran); and Bimeh Markasi-Central Insurance of Iran (CII, Iran)	Sanctioned. Under amendments to ISA by Iran Threat Reduction Act sanctioning owning vessels that transport Iranian oil or providing insurance for the shipments. Treasury sanctions also imposed on these and eight UAE-based oil graders that concealed the transactions.
April 12, 2013	Tanker Pacific; SAMAMA; and Allvale Maritime	Sanctions lifted. Special rule applied after firms provided to the U.S. "reliable assurances" they will not engage in sanctionable activities in the future.
May 31, 2013	Ferland Co. Ltd. (Cyprus and Ukraine)	Sanctioned. For cooperating with National Iranian Tanker Co. to illicitly sell Iranian crude oil. Sanctions also imposed by Treasury under E.O. 13608.

Source: State Department announcements.

Sanctions on Oil and Other Payments to Iran's Central Bank

In late 2011, some in Congress believed that action was needed to cut off the mechanisms oil importers use to pay Iran hard currency for oil. Proposals to cut Iran's Central Bank from the international financial system were based on that objective, as well as on the view that the Central Bank helps other Iranian banks circumvent the U.S. and U.N. banking pressure.

In November 2011, provisions to sanction foreign banks that deal with Iran's Central Bank were incorporated into a FY2012 national defense authorization bill (H.R. 1540, signed on December 31, 2011 [P.L. 112-81]). Section 1245 of P.L. 112-81 provides for the following:

- Requires the President to prevent a foreign bank from opening an account in the United States—or impose strict limitations on existing U.S. accounts—if that bank processes payments through Iran's Central Bank.

- *Exemption Provision.* Foreign banks can be granted an exemption from sanctions (for any transactions with the Central Bank, not just for oil) if the President certifies that the parent country of the bank has *significantly reduced* its purchases of oil from Iran. That determination is reviewed every 180 days; countries must continue to reduce their oil buys from Iran, relative to the previous 180-day period, to retain the exemption.

- *Effective Dates.* The provision applied to *non-oil related* transactions with the Central Bank of Iran 60 days after enactment (by February 29, 2012). The provision applied to transactions with the Central Bank for *oil purchases* only after 180 days (as of June 28, 2012).

- The provision applies to a foreign central bank only if the transaction with Iran's Central Bank is for oil purchases.

- Sanctions on transactions for oil apply only if the President certifies to Congress—90 days after enactment (by March 30, 2012), based on a report by the Energy Information Administration to be completed 60 days after enactment (by February 29, 2012)—that the oil market *is* adequately supplied. The EIA report and Administration certification are required every 90 days thereafter.

Although Treasury Under Secretary David Cohen told the Senate Foreign Relations Committee on December 2, 2011, that the provision could lead to a rise in oil prices that would benefit Iran, the Administration accepted the legislation. In the signing statement on the bill, President Obama indicated he would implement the provision so as not to damage U.S. relations with partner countries.

Waiver and Termination Provisions

The law provides for the President to waive the sanctions for 120 days, renewable for successive 120 day periods, if the President determines that doing so is in the national security interest.

The Administration has the authority to grant exceptions, as stipulated, but outright repeal or amendment of this law would require congressional action.

This provision was waived on January 20, 2014, in order to implement the JPA, meaning that Iran's oil customers will not be required to further reduce oil purchases from Iran during the JPA period. Iran is demanding that this sanction no longer apply as part of a comprehensive nuclear deal, and the United States and its partners are likely to agree to suspend or lift this sanction as part of a comprehensive nuclear deal.

Implementation: Exemptions Issued

On February 27, 2012, the Department of the Treasury announced regulations to implement Section 1245. The first required EIA report was issued on February 29, 2012, and, on March 30,

2012, President Obama determined that there was a sufficient supply of oil worldwide to permit countries to reduce oil purchases from Iran. An EIA report of April 27, 2012, and Administration determination of June 11, 2012, made similar findings and certifications, triggering potential sanctions as of June 28, 2012. Subsequent EIA reports and Administration determinations of the state of the oil market have kept the sanctions triggers in place.

The lack of precise definition of "significant reduction" in oil purchases gives the Administration flexibility in applying the exemption provision. On January 19, 2012, several Senators wrote to Treasury Secretary Geithner agreeing with outside experts that the Treasury Department should define "significant reduction" as an 18% purchase reduction based on total price paid (not just volumes).[19] Administration officials said they largely adopted that standard. P.L. 112-158 also amended Section 1245 such that any country that has received an exemption would retain that exemption if it completely ceases purchasing oil from Iran. The EU embargo on purchases of Iranian oil, announced January 23, 2012, and which took full effect by July 1, 2012, implied that virtually all EU oil customers of Iran would obtain exemptions. The table below on major Iranian oil customers indicates cuts made by major customers compared to 2011.

Exemptions Issued[20]

- On March 20, 2012, the Secretary of State announced the first group of 11 countries that had achieved an exemption for significantly reducing oil purchases from Iran: Belgium, the Czech Republic, France, Germany, Greece, Italy, Japan, the Netherlands, Poland, Spain, and Britain. The exemptions for these 11 countries have all been renewed since. (Seventeen EU countries were not granted exemptions because they were not buying Iran's oil and could not "significantly reduce" buys from Iran.)

- On June 11, 2012, the Administration granted seven more exemptions based on reductions of oil purchases from Iran of about 20% in each case: India, Korea, Turkey, Malaysia, South Africa, Sri Lanka, and Taiwan. All have been renewed since.

- On June 28, 2012, the Administration granted exemptions to China and Singapore, two remaining major Iran oil customers, with China the single largest buyer. The exemptions were renewed repeatedly since.

Sanctions on Paying Iran with Hard Currency

The ability of Iran to acquire hard currency has been further impeded by a provision of the Iran Threat Reduction Act (P.L. 112-158), which went into effect on February 6, 2013—180 days after enactment. Section 504 of the Iran Threat Reduction Act amended P.L. 112-81 (adding "clause ii" to Paragraph D(1)) by requiring that any funds owed to Iran as a result of exempted transactions (oil purchases, for example) be credited to an account located in the country with primary jurisdiction over the foreign bank making the transaction. This has the net effect of preventing Iran from bringing earned hard currency back to Iran and compelling it to buy the products of the oil customer countries.

[19] Text of letter from Senators Mark Kirk and Robert Menendez to Secretary Geithner, January 19, 2012.

[20] Announcements by the Department of State, March 20, 2012, June 11, 2012, and June 28, 2012.

Waiver Provision

The waiver provision that applies to the sanctions to be imposed under the FY2012 NDAA (P.L. 112-81) applies to this hard currency "lock-up" provision.

To implement the JPA, a waiver was issued under P.L. 112-81 to allow Iran to receive some hard currency from ongoing oil sales in eight installments during the JPA period. Iran remains unable, even under the JPA, to remove hard currency from existing accounts abroad. Iran is likely to demand that this sanction be lifted as part of a comprehensive nuclear deal so that Iran can access its hard currency accounts abroad unfettered.

Table 2. Top Energy Buyers From Iran and Reductions

(amounts in barrels per day, bpd)

Country/Bloc	2011 Average	Average (at time of JPA implementation start)
European Union (particularly Italy, Spain, and Greece)	600,000	Negligible
China	550,000	410,000
Japan	325,000	190,000
India	320,000	190,000
South Korea	230,000	130,000
Turkey	200,000	120,000
South Africa	80,000	Negligible
Malaysia	55,000	Negligible
Sri Lanka	35,000	Negligible
Taiwan	35,000	10,000
Singapore	20,000	Negligible
Other	55,000	Negligible
Total	**2.5 mbd**	**1.057 mbd**

Source: International Energy Agency and rough estimates based on CRS conversations with foreign diplomats and press reports.

Note: Actual volumes might differ, and import volumes may fluctuate dramatically over short periods of time as actual tanker deliveries occur.

Proliferation-Related Sanctions

Aside from the "terrorism list sanctions" discussed above, several laws and executive orders seek to bars Iran from obtaining U.S. or other technology that can be used for weapons of mass destruction programs (WMD).

Iran-Iraq Arms Nonproliferation Act and Iraq Sanctions Act

The Iran-Iraq Arms Nonproliferation Act (P.L. 102-484, signed in October 1992) imposes a number of sanctions on foreign entities that supply Iran with WMD technology or "destabilizing numbers and types of advanced conventional weapons." Sanctions imposed on violating entities include a ban, for two years, on U.S. government procurement from that entity, and a two-year ban on licensing U.S. exports to that entity. A sanction to ban imports to the United States from the entity is authorized.

If the violator is determined to be a foreign country, sanctions to be imposed are a one-year ban on U.S. assistance to that country; a one-year requirement that the United States vote against international lending to it; a one-year suspension of U.S. co-production agreements with the country; a one-year suspension of technical exchanges with the country in military or dual use technology; and a one-year ban on sales of U.S. arms to the country. The President is also authorized to deny the country most-favored-nation trade status; and to impose a ban on U.S. trade with the country.

Section 1603 of the act amends an earlier law, the Iraq Sanctions Act of 1990 (Section 586G(a) of P.L. 101-513) also provides for a "presumption of denial" for all dual use exports to Iran (which would include computer software).

Waiver and Termination

Section 1606 of the Act provides a presidential waiver for the provisions of the Act, and for those imposed pursuant to the Iraq Sanctions Act of 1990, if the President determines a waiver is "essential to the national interest."

Terminating this sanction outright would require congressional action. It is not clear whether this sanction will be lifted or waived as part of a comprehensive nuclear deal.

Iran-North Korea-Syria Nonproliferation Act

The Iran Nonproliferation Act (P.L. 106-178, signed in March 2000) is now called the Iran-North Korea-Syria Non-Proliferation Act (INKSNA) after amendments applying its provisions to North Korea and to Syria. It authorizes sanctions on foreign *persons* (individuals or corporations, not countries or governments) that are determined by the Administration to have assisted Iran's WMD programs. Sanctions imposed include a prohibition on U.S. exportation of arms and dual use items to the sanctioned entity, and, under Executive Order 12938 (of November 14, 1994), a ban on U.S. government procurement and of imports to the United States from the sanctioned entity. The law also bans U.S. extraordinary payments to the Russian Aviation and Space Agency in connection with the international space station unless the President can certify that the agency or entities under its control had not transferred any WMD or missile technology to Iran within the year prior.[21] (A continuing resolution for FY2009, which funded the U.S. government through March 2009, waived this law to allow NASA to continue to use Russian vehicles to access the International Space Station.)

Implementation: Entities sanctioned under this law are listed in the tables at the end of the report.

---

[21] The provision contains certain exceptions to ensure the safety of astronauts, but it nonetheless threatened to limit U.S. access to the international space station after April 2006, when Russia started charging the United States for transportation on its Soyuz spacecraft. Legislation in the 109th Congress (S. 1713, P.L. 109-112) amended the provision in order to facilitate continued U.S. access and extended INA sanctions provisions to Syria.

Waiver and Termination

Section 4 gives the President the authority to not impose sanctions if the President justifies that decision to Congress. Section 5 provides for exemptions from sanctions if certain conditions are met, particularly that the government with jurisdiction over the entity cooperating to stop future such transfers to Iran.

Termination of this law outright would require congressional action.

Executive Order 13382

Executive Order 13382 (June 28, 2005) allows the President to block the assets of proliferators of weapons of mass destruction (WMD) and their supporters under the authority granted by the International Emergency Economic Powers Act (IEEPA; 50 U.S.C. 1701 et seq.), the National Emergencies Act (50 U.S.C. 1601 et seq.), and Section 301 of Title 3, *United States Code*.

Implementation. The numerous entities sanctioned under the order for dealings with Iran are listed in the tables at the end of this report.

Foreign Aid Restrictions for Suppliers of Iran

Successive foreign aid appropriations have withheld 60% of any U.S. assistance to the Russian Federation unless it terminates technical assistance to Iran's nuclear and ballistic missiles programs. Because U.S. aid to Russia generally goes directly to programs in Russia and not to the Russian government, little or no funding has been withheld as a result of the provision.

Sanctions on "Countries of Diversion Concern"

Title III of CISADA established authorities to sanction countries that allow U.S. technology that Iran could use in its nuclear and WMD programs to be re-exported or diverted to Iran. Section 303 of CISADA authorizes the President to designate a country as a "Destination of Diversion Concern" if that country allows substantial diversion of goods, services, or technologies characterized in Section 302 of that law to Iranian end-users or Iranian intermediaries. The technologies specified include any goods that could contribute to Iran's nuclear or WMD programs, as well as goods listed on various U.S. controlled-technology lists such as the Comerce Control List or Munitions List. For any country designated as a country of diversion concern, there would be prohibition of denial for licenses of U.S. exports to that country of the goods that were being re-exported or diverted to Iran.

Implementation: No country has been designated a "Country of Diversion Concern."

Waiver and Termination

Waiver: The President may waive sanctions on countries designated as of Diversion Concern for 12 months, and additional 12 month periods, pursuant to certification that the country is taking steps to prevent such diversions and re-exports.

Termination: The designation terminates on the date the President certifies to Congress that the country has adequately strengthened its export controls to prevent such diversion and re-exports to Iran in the future.

Sanctions on the Islamic Revolutionary Guard Corps (IRGC)

Numerous sanctions discussed in this report target Iran's Islamic Revolutionary Guard Corps (IRGC), which plays a role in repressing domestic dissent, developing Iran's energy sector, developing Iran's WMD programs particularly by procuring technology abroad, and supporting pro-Iranian militant movements and governments in the Middle East region. Much of the work on Iran's oil and gas fields is done through a series of contractors. Some of them, such as Khatam ol-Anbia and Oriental Kish, have been identified by the U.S. government as controlled by the IRGC and have been sanctioned under various executive orders, discussed below. The 2011 appointment of Khatam ol-Anbia's chief, Rostam Ghasemi, as oil minister, caused the U.S. government and many experts to assess that the IRGC role in Iran's energy sector was large and growing. He was replaced by President Hassan Rouhani with a former Oil Minister and oil industry professional, but the IRGC involvement in Iran's energy sector is not shrinking. The *Wall Street Journal* reported on May 27, 2014, that Khatam ol-Anbia has $50 billion in contracts with the Iranian government, including in the energy sector but also in port and highway construction. It has as many as 40,000 employees. Sanctions targeting the IRGC are discussed below:

- Section 311 of the Iran Threat Reduction Act requires a certification by a contractor to the U.S. government that it is not knowingly engaging in a significant transaction with Iran's Islamic Revolutionary Guard Corps (IRGC), or any of its agents or affiliates that have been sanctioned under several executive orders discussed below. A contract may be terminated if it is determined that the company's certification of compliance was false.

- Section 302 of the Iran Threat Reduction Act imposes at least 5 out of 12 ISA sanctions on persons that materially assist, with financing or technology, the IRGC, or assist or engage in "significant" transactions with any of its affiliates that are sanctioned under Executive Order 13382, 13224, or similar executive orders discussed below—or which are determined to be affiliates of the IRGC. *Section 302 did not amend ISA.*

- Section 301 of the Iran Threat Reduction Act requires the President, within 90 days of enactment (by November 9, 2012), to identify "officials, agents, or affiliates" of the IRGC and to impose sanctions in accordance with Executive Order 13382 or 13224, including blocking any such designee's U.S.-based assets or property. Some of these designations, including of National Iranian Oil Company (NIOC), were made by Treasury Department on November 8, 2012.

- Section 303 of the Iran Threat Reduction Act requires the imposition of sanctions on agencies of foreign governments that provide technical or financial support, or goods and services to sanctioned (under U.S. executive orders or U.N. resolutions) members or affiliates of the IRGC. Sanctions include a ban on U.S. assistance or credits for that foreign government agency, a ban on defense sales to it, a ban on U.S. arms sales to it, and a ban on exports to it of controlled U.S. technology.

- Section 104 of CISADA sanctions foreign banks that conduct significant transactions with the IRGC or any of its agents or affiliates that are sanctioned under any executive order. It also sanctions any entity that assists Iran's Central Bank efforts to help the IRGC acquire WMD or support international terrorism.

- The IRGC is named as a proliferation supporting entity under Executive Order 13382, and the Qods Force, the unit of the IRGC that assists pro-Iranian movements and countries abroad, is named as a terrorism supporting entity under Executive Order 13324. Several Iranian firms linked to the IRGC are sanctioned, as noted in the tables at the end of this report. Several IRGC commanders are named under other executive orders, discussed below, sanctioning Iranian human rights abusers, abusers of Syrian human rights, and entities undermining stability in Iraq.

- No IRGC-related laws or executive orders were required to be waived or suspended to implement the JPA.

Financial/Banking Sanctions

U.S. efforts to shut Iran out of the international banking system have gained strength as other countries have joined the effort. These efforts have been implemented primarily by the Treasury

---

Department through progressively strong actions, particularly using the authority in legislation in 2011 to cut off Iran's Central Bank from the international financial system.

Early Efforts: Targeted Financial Measures

Since 2006, the Treasury Department has used existing authorities to persuade foreign banks to cease dealing with Iran by attempting to convince the banks that Iran is using the international financial system to fund terrorist groups and acquire weapons-related technology. According to a GAO report of February 2013, the Treasury Department made overtures to 145 banks in 60 countries, including several visits to banks and officials in the UAE, and convinced at least 80 foreign banks to cease handling financial transactions with Iranian banks. In November 6, 2008, the Treasury Department has barred U.S. banks from handling any indirect transactions ("U-turn transactions," meaning transactions with non-Iranian foreign banks that are handling transactions on behalf of an Iranian bank) with all Iranian banks.[22]

Implementation: The Treasury Department also used punishments against banks that have helped Iran violate U.S. financial restrictions. In 2004, the Treasury Department fined UBS $100 million for the unauthorized movement of U.S. dollars to Iran and other sanctioned countries. In December 2005, the Treasury Department fined Dutch bank ABN Amro $80 million for failing to fully report the processing of financial transactions involving Iran's Bank Melli (and another bank partially owned by Libya). In December 2009, Credit Suisse agreed to pay $536 million for illicit processing of Iranian transactions with U.S. banks. In June 2012, Dutch bank IMG agreed to pay $619 million for moving billions of dollars through the U.S. financial system, using falsified records, on behalf of Iranian and Cuban clients. Standard Chartered agreed in August 2012 to a $340 million settlement with New York State regulators for allegedly processing transactions with Iran in contravention of U.S. regulations.[23] In January 2014, Clearstream Banking, based in Luxembourg, agree to pay $152 million for permitting Iran to evade restrictions on dealing with U.S. banks. That same month, the Bank of Moscow agreed to pay $9.5 million for illicitly moving money through the U.S. financial system on behalf of Bank Melli.[24] On June 30, 2014, BNP Paribas paid an unprecedented $9 billion in fines for helping Iran, Sudan, and Cuba violate U.S. sanctions.

CISADA: Sanctioning Foreign Banks That Conduct Transactions with Iran

The Treasury Department efforts were enhanced substantially by Section 104 of CISADA (P.L. 111-195) and U.N. and EU sanctions. The intent of Section 104 was to weaken Iran's economy by preventing Iranian traders from obtaining "letters of credit" (trade financing) to buy or sell goods. The binding provisions of Section 104 of CISADA require the Secretary of the Treasury to prescribe several sets of regulations to forbid U.S. banks from opening new "correspondent accounts" or "payable-through accounts" (or force the cancellation of existing such accounts) for foreign banks that process "significant transactions" with

---

[22] Glenn Kessler, "U.S. Moves to Isolate Iranian Banks," *Washington Post*, September 9, 2006.

[23] Jessica Silver-Greenberg, "Regulator Says Bank Helped Iran Hide Deals," *New York Times*, August 7, 2012.

[24] Rick Gladstone. "U.S. Announces Actions to Enforce Iran Sanctions." *New York Times*, April 29, 2014.

- Any foreign entity that is sanctioned by Executive Order 13224 or 13382 (terrorism and proliferation activities, respectively). These orders are discussed elsewhere in this report. To date, several hundred entities (including individuals), many of them Iran-based or of Iranian origin, have been sanctioned under these two Orders; a full list is at the end of this report.

- Any entity designated under by U.N. Security Council resolutions that impose sanctions on Iran.

- Iran's energy, shipping, and shipbuilding sectors, including with NIOC, NITC, and IRISL. (This provision was added by Section 1244(d) of the FY2013 National Defense Authorization Act (P.L. 112-239) *but it does not specifically amend CISADA*).

Foreign banks that do not have operations in the United States typically establish correspondent accounts or payable-through accounts with U.S. banks as a means of accessing the U.S. financial system. The Treasury Department has authority to determine what constitutes a "significant" financial transaction.

Implementation of Section 104: Sanctions Imposed

On July 31, 2012, the Administration announced the first sanctions under Section 104 of CISADA. Sanctioned were the Bank of Kunlun in China and the Elaf Islamic Bank in Iraq. However, on May 17, 2013, the Treasury Department lifted sanctions on Elaf Islamic Bank in Iraq, asserting that the bank had reduced its exposure to the Iranian financial sector and stopped providing services to an Iranian bank sanctioned by the EU (Export Development Bank of Iran).

Waiver and Termination

Under Section 401(a) of CISADA, the Section 104 sanctions provisions would terminate 30 days after the President certifies to Congress that Iran (1) has met the requirements for removal from the terrorism list, AND (2) has ceased pursuit, acquisition or development of, and verifiably dismantled its nuclear weapons and other WMD programs.

The Secretary of the Treasury may waive sanctions under Section 104, with the waiver taking effect 30 days after the Secretary determines that a waiver is necessary to the national interest and submits a report to Congress describing the reason for that determination.

Waivers of CISADA were not required to implement the JPA. Iran is likely to demand that this sanction no longer apply after any comprehensive nuclear deal.

Iran Designated a Money-Laundering Jurisdiction

On November 21, 2011, the Administration took further steps to isolate Iran's banking system by identifying Iran as a "jurisdiction of primary money laundering concern"[25] under Section 311 of the USA Patriot Act (31 U.S.C. 5318A). The Treasury Department determined that Iran's financial system, including the Central Bank, constitutes a threat to governments or financial institutions that do business with these banks. The designation carried no immediate penalty, but

---

[25] http://www.treasury.gov/press-center/press-releases/Pages/tg1367.aspx.

it imposed additional requirements on U.S. banks to ensure against improper Iranian access to the U.S. financial system.

Promoting Divestment

A recent trend in Congress and in several states has been to require or call for divestment of shares of firms that have invested in Iran's energy sector at the levels sanctionable under ISA.[26] The intent of doing so is to express the view of Western and other democracies that Iran is an outcast internationally. A divestment provision was contained in CISADA, providing a "safe harbor" for investment managers who sell shares of firms that invest in Iran's energy sector.

Section 219 of the Iran Threat Reduction and Syria Human Rights Act of 2012 requires companies, in their reports to the Securities and Exchange Commission, to disclose whether it or any corporate affiliate has engaged in any sanctionable transactions with Iran under ISA, CISADA, and other applicable laws.

Sanctions and Sanctions Exemptions to Support Democratic Change/Civil Society in Iran

A trend in U.S. policy and legislation since the June 12, 2009, election-related uprising in Iran has been to support the ability of the domestic opposition in Iran to communicate, to reduce the regime's ability to monitor or censor Internet communications, and to sanction Iranian officials that commit human rights abuses. Sanctions on the IRGC (see box above) represent one facet of that trend because the IRGC is not only involved in Iran's WMD programs but it is also the key instrument through which the regime has suppressed oppositionists. Earlier, the Iran Freedom Support Act (IFSA; P.L. 109-293) authorized "sums as may be necessary" to assist Iranians who are "dedicated" to "democratic values ... and the adoption of a democratic form of government in Iran"; and "advocates the adherence by Iran to nonproliferation regimes."

General Implementation: Individuals and entities designated under the Executive Orders and provisions discussed below are listed in the tables at the end of this report. For those provisions that ban visas to enter the United States, the State Department interprets the provisions to apply to all members of the designated entity.[27] Similar sanctions against many of these same officials—as well as several others—have been imposed by the European Union.

No suspension of U.S. sanctions on Iran for its human rights practices was required by the JPA. U.S. statements indicate that sanctions related specifically to human rights issues will not be eased as part of a comprehensive nuclear settlement, if reached.

---

[26] For information on the steps taken by individual states, see National Conference of State Legislatures, "State Divestment Legislation."

[27] U.S. Department of the Treasury, Office of Public Affairs, *Treasury Sanctions Iranian Security Forces for Human Rights Abuses*, June 9, 2011.

Expanding Internet and Communications Freedoms

Some laws and Administration action focus on expanding Internet freedom in Iran or preventing the Iranian government from using the Internet to identify opponents. Subtitle D of the FY2010 Defense Authorization Act (P.L. 111-84), called the "VOICE" (Victims of Iranian Censorship) Act contained several provisions to increase U.S. broadcasting to Iran and to identify (in a report to be submitted 180 days after enactment) companies that are selling Iran technology equipment that it can use to suppress or monitor the Internet usage of Iranians. The act authorized funds to document Iranian human rights abuses since the June 2009 presidential election. Section 1241 of the act also required an Administration report by January 31, 2010, on U.S. enforcement of sanctions against Iran, and the effect of those sanctions on Iran.

Sanctions and Administrative Actions Against Iran's Internet Censorship

The "Reduce Iranian Cyber-Suppression Act" (111th Congress, S. 1475 and H.R. 3284) was incorporated into CISADA as Section 106. The section prohibits U.S. government contracts with foreign companies that sell technology that Iran could use to monitor or control Iranian usage of the Internet. The provisions were directed, in part, against a joint venture between Nokia (Finland) and Siemens (Germany) that reportedly sold Internet monitoring and censorship technology to Iran in 2008.[28] Section 103(b)(2) of CISADA exempts from the U.S. export ban on Iran equipment to help Iranians communicate and use the Internet.

Section 403 of the Iran Threat Reduction and Syria Human Rights Act (P.L. 112-158, August 2010) sanctions (visa ban, U.S.-based property blocked) persons/firms determined to have engaged in censorship in Iran, limited access to media, or—for example, a foreign satellite service provider—supported Iranian government jamming or frequency manipulation.

The Administration took several separate steps to facilitate Internet communications among Iranians.

- On March 8, 2010, OFAC amended the Iran Transactions Regulations to provide for a general license for providing to Iranians free mass market software in order to. The ruling incorporated major features of the Iran Digital Empowerment Act (H.R. 4301 in the 111th Congress). The OFAC determination required a waiver of the provision of the Iran-Iraq Arms Nonproliferation Act (Section 1606 waiver provision) discussed above.

- On March 20, 2012, the Treasury Department announced that several additional types of software and information technology products would be able to be exported to Iran under general license, including personal communications, personal data storage, browsers, plug-ins, document readers, and free mobile applications related to personal communications. The exports could proceed provided the products were available at no cost to the user.[29] On May 30, 2013, the Treasury Department further amended its policies to allow for the sale, *on a cash basis* (no U.S. financing), to Iran of equipment (e.g., cellphones, laptops,

---

[28] Christopher Rhoads, "Iran's Web Spying Aided by Western Technology," *Wall Street Journal*, June 22, 2009.

[29] *Fact Sheet: Treasury Issues Interpretive Guidance and Statement of Licensing Policy on Internet Freedom in Iran*, March 20, 2012.

satellite Internet, website hosting, and related products and services) that Iranians can use to communicate.

- On April 23, 2012, President Obama issued an executive order (13606) directly addressing the issue by sanctioning persons who commit "Grave Human Rights Abuses by the Governments of Iran and Syria Via Information Technology (GHRAVITY)." The order blocks the U.S.-based property and essentially bars U.S. entry and bans any U.S. trade with persons and entities listed in an Annex and persons or entities subsequently determined to be (1) operating any technology that allows the Iranian (or Syrian) government to disrupt, monitor, or track computer usage by citizens of those countries or assisting the two governments in such disruptions or monitoring; or (2) selling to Iran (or Syria) any technology that enables those governments to carry out such disruptions or monitoring.

- On October 9, 2012, the President issued Executive Order 13628 reinforcing Section 403 of the Iran Threat Reduction Act by blocking the property of persons/firms determined to have committed the censorship, limited free expression, or assisted in jamming communications. The Order also specifies the authorities of the Department of State and the Department of the Treasury to impose sanctions.

Measures to Sanction Human Rights Abuses and Promote the Opposition

Another part of the effort to help Iran's opposition has been legislation to sanction regime officials involved in suppressing the domestic opposition in Iran. The following sections discuss sanctions against Iran's human rights abuses.

Sanctions Against Iranian Human Rights Abusers and Related Equipment

Section 105 of CISADA was modeled on a Senate bill, S. 3022, the Iran Human Rights Sanctions Act, in the 111th Congress. The section bans travel and freezing assets of those Iranians determined to be human rights abusers. On September 29, 2010, pursuant to Section 105, President Obama signed an Executive Order (13553) providing for the CISADA sanctions against Iranians determined to be responsible for or complicit in post-2009 Iran election human rights abuses. Those named under the provisions are listed in the tables at the end of this report.

Termination Authority

Section 105 contains its own specific authority to terminate the section through Administration action. Section 105 can be terminated if the President certifies to Congress that Iran has (1) unconditionally released all political prisoners detained in the aftermath of the June 2009 uprising; (2) ceased its practices of violence, unlawful detention, torture, and abuse of citizens who were engaged in peaceful protest; (3) fully investigated abuses of political activists that occurred after the uprising; and (4) committed to and is making progress toward establishing an independent judiciary and respecting human rights recognized in the Universal Declaration of Human Rights.

Sales of Anti-Riot Equipment

Section 402 of the Iran Threat Reduction and Syria Human Rights Act of 2012 (P.L. 112-158) amended Section 105 by adding provisions that sanctions (visa ban, U.S. property blocked) for any person or company that sells the Iranian government goods or technologies that it can use to commit human rights abuses against its people. Such goods include firearms, rubber bullets, police batons, chemical or pepper sprays, stun grenades, tear gas, water cannons, and like goods. Under that section, ISA sanctions are additionally to be imposed on any person determined to be selling such equipment to the IRGC.

Sanctions Against Iranian Broadcasting and Profiteers

IFCA (Subtitle D of P.L. 112-239), Section 1248, mandates inclusion of the Islamic Republic of Iran Broadcasting (IRIB), the state broadcasting umbrella group, as a human rights abuser, thereby imposing CISADA Section 105 sanctions (travel ban, asset freeze) on that entity.

Section 1249 amends CISADA by making sanctionable under Section 105 any person determined to have engaged in corruption or to have diverted or misappropriated humanitarian goods or funds for such goods for the Iranian people. The measure is intended to sanction Iranian profiteers who are, for example, using official connections to corner the market for vital medicines. This essentially codifies a similar provision of Executive Order 13645.

Separate Visa Ban

On July 8, 2011, the State Department imposed visa restrictions on more than 50 Iranian officials for participating in political repression in Iran. The State Department announcement stated that the names of those subject to the ban would not be released because visa records are confidential. The action was taken under the authorities of Section 212(a)(3)(C) of the Immigration and Nationality Act, which renders inadmissible to the United States a foreign person whose activities could have serious consequences for the United States. On May 30, 2013, the State Department announced it had imposed visa restrictions on an additional 60 Iranian officials and other individuals who participated in human rights abuses related to political repression in Iran.[30]

There are certain exemptions in the case of high level Iranian visits to attend the United Nations. Under the U.N. Participation Act (P.L. 79-264) that provides for U.S. participation in the United Nations and as host nation of U.N. headquarters in New York, visas are routinely issued to heads of state and members of their entourage attending these meetings. In September 2012, however, the State Department refused visas for 20 members of Iranian President Ahmadinejad's traveling party on the grounds of past involvement in terrorism or human rights abuses. Still, in line with U.S. obligations under the act, then President Ahmadinejad was allowed to fly to the United States on Iran Air, even though Iran Air is a U.S.-sanctioned entity, and his plane reportedly was allowed to stay at Andrews Air Force base for the duration of his visit.

[30] http://www.state.gov/r/pa/prs/ps/2013/05/210102 htm.

U.N. Sanctions

U.N. sanctions apply to all U.N. member states. As part of a multilateral process of attempting to convince Iran to choose the path of negotiations or face further penalty, during 2006-2008, three U.N. Security Council resolutions—1737, 1747, and 1803—imposed sanctions primarily on Iran's weapons of mass destruction (WMD) infrastructure. Resolution 1929 was adopted on June 9, 2010, by a vote of 12-2 (Turkey and Brazil), with one abstention (Lebanon). (Iranian entities and persons under U.N. sanctions are in **Table 5**.) A summary of the major provisions of all four of these resolutions is contained in the table below.

U.N. Security Council action was not needed to implement the JPA. The JPA makes reference to a comprehensive settlement satisfying all provisions of U.N. resolutions on Iran, indicating that Security Council action might be taken to implement any comprehensive agreement.

Table 3. Summary of Provisions of U.N. Resolutions on Iran Nuclear Program (1737, 1747, 1803, and 1929)

Requires Iran to suspend uranium enrichment, to suspend construction of the heavy-water reactor at Arak, ratify the "Additional Protocol" to Iran's IAEA Safeguards Agreement. (1737)

Freezes the assets of Iranian persons and entities named in annexes to the resolutions, and requires that countries ban the travel of named Iranians. (1737, 1747, 1803, and 1929)

Prohibits transfer to Iran of nuclear, missile, and dual use items to Iran, except for use in light-water reactors. (1737, and 1747)

Prohibits Iran from exporting arms or WMD-useful technology (1747)

Prohibits Iran from investing abroad in uranium mining, related nuclear technologies or nuclear capable ballistic missile technology, and prohibits Iran from launching ballistic missiles (including on its territory). (1929)

Requires Iran to refrain from any development of ballistic missiles that are nuclear capable. (1929)

Mandates that countries not export major combat systems to Iran, but does not bar sales of missiles that are not on the U.N. Registry of Conventional Arms. (1929)

Calls for voluntary restraint on transactions with Iranian banks, particularly Bank Melli and Bank Saderat. (1929)

Calls for vigilance on international lending to Iran and providing trade credits and other financing. (1929)

Calls on countries to inspect cargoes carried by Iran Air Cargo and Islamic Republic of Iran Shipping Lines—or by any ships in national or international waters—if there are indications they carry cargo banned for carriage to Iran. Searches in international waters would require concurrence of the country where the ship is registered. (1929)

A Sanctions Committee, composed of the 15 members of the Security Council, monitors implementation of all Iran sanctions and collects and disseminates information on Iranian violations and other entities involved in banned activities. A "panel of experts" is empowered by 1929 to assist the U.N. sanctions committee in implementing the resolution and previous Iran resolutions, and to suggest ways of more effective implementation.

Source: Text of U.N. Security Council resolutions 1737, 1747, 1803, and 1929. http://www.un.org. More information on specific provisions of each of these resolutions and the nuclear negotiations with Iran is in CRS Report RL32048, *Iran: U.S. Concerns and Policy Responses*, by Kenneth Katzman.

International Implementation and Compliance[31]

During 2010-2013, converging international views on Iran produced substantial global cooperation in pressuring Iran with sanctions—including among Iran's neighbors that are often reluctant to antagonize Iran. Some countries apparently joined the sanctions regime primarily as a means of heading off unwanted military action against Iran by the United States or by Israel. U.S. officials say they expect that same degree of cooperation with respect to the Joint Plan of Action—both in easing sanctions temporarily and in preventing an easing beyond that stipulated by the JPA. The JPA—which ran from January 20, 2014, until July 20, 2014, and was extended until November 24, 2014—requires Iran's oil exports to remain constant (about 1 million barrels per day). Iran's oil customers are not required to cut average purchases further but are not permitted to increase those purchases either.

A comparison between U.S., U.N., and EU sanctions against Iran is contained in **Table 4** below. To increase international compliance with all applicable sanctions, on May 1, 2012, President Obama issued Executive Order 13608, giving the Treasury Department the ability to identify and sanction (cutting them off from the U.S. market) foreign persons who help Iran (or Syria) evade U.S. and multilateral sanctions.

The United States and its partners have also sought to stop Iran from using traditional trading patterns common to its neighborhood to evade sanctions. On January 10, 2013, the Treasury Department's Office of Foreign Assets Control issued an Advisory to highlight Iran's use of *hawalas* (traditional informal banking and money exchanges) in the Middle East and South Asia region to circumvent financial sanctions. U.S. and other banks sometimes process *hawala* transactions involving Iranian entities because the *hawalas* are able to conceal the Iranian involvement.

Europe

U.S. and European approaches on Iran have converged the nuclear issue came to the fore in 2002. Previously, European and other countries appeared less concerned than is the United States about Iran's support for militant movements in the Middle East or Iran's strategic power in the Persian Gulf and were reluctant to sanction Iran. Since the passage of Resolution 1929 in June 2010, European Union (EU) sanctions on Iran have become nearly as extensive as those of the United States. The EU is a party to the JPA, and, as of January 20, 2014, the EU is implementing easing of those sanctions below—unless specified otherwise. EU sanctions are as follows.

- A ban on EU oil imports from Iran went into effect on July 1, 2012, pursuant to a January 23, 2012, EU decision. Collectively, the EU bought about 600,000 barrels per day of Iranian oil in 2011, about a quarter of Iran's total oil exports. The embargo was imposed despite the fact that the most vulnerable EU economies—Spain, Italy, and Greece—were each buying more than 10% of their oil from Iran. Because of the embargo, 10 EU countries have maintained

---

[31] Note: CRS has no mandate or capability to "judge" compliance of any country with U.S., multilateral, or international sanctions against Iran. This section is intended to analyze some major trends in third country cooperation with U.S. policy toward Iran. These assessments bear in mind that there are many other issues and considerations in U.S. relations with the countries discussed here.

exemptions from sanctions under (P.L. 112-81). A ban on EU imports of natural gas from Iran went into effect in October 2012 and intended to stall Iran's efforts to expand gas exports to Europe. *The sanctions relief in the JPA has not altered the EU ban on imports of oil or gas from Iran.*

- An EU ban on insurance for shipping oil or petrochemicals from Iran took full effect on July 1, 2012. Earlier, most EU-based insurers closed their offices in Iran.

- The EU has banned all trade with Iran in gold, precious metals, diamonds, and petrochemical products.

- The EU has frozen the assets of Iran's Central Bank, although transactions are still be permitted for approved legitimate trade, and it froze the assets of several Iranian firms involved in shipping arms to Syria or which support shipping by IRISL, and cease doing business with port operator Tidewater (see above). *This sanction has not been eased to implement the JPA.*

- As of October 15, 2012, there has been a ban on transactions between European and all Iranian banks, unless specifically authorized.

- The EU has banned short-term export credits, guarantees, and insurance.

- The EU has banned exports to Iran of graphite, semi-finished metals such as aluminum and steel, industrial software, shipbuilding technology, oil storage capabilities, and flagging or classification services for Iranian tankers and cargo vessels. *With the exception of exports to Iran's automotive sector, the EU ban on export of these technologies was not suspended.*

SWIFT Cutoff. Section 220 of P.L. 112-158 requires reports on electronic payments systems such as the Brussels-based SWIFT (Society of Worldwide Interbank Financial Telecommunications) that might be doing business with Iran, but does not mandate sanctions against such systems. The EU reacted to that legislation by requesting that SWIFT cut off sanctioned Iranian banks from the network. SWIFT acceded to that request on March 17, 2012, denying access to 14 Iranian banks blacklisted by the EU. The United States has sanctioned about 50 Iranian banks, but those not sanctioned by the EU apparently can still access the SWIFT system.[32] And, some experts report that Iranian banks are still able to conduct electronic transactions with the European Central Bank via an electronic payments system called "Target II." The *SWIFT sanctions have not been suspended to implement the JPA. Most experts assess that Iran will demand that this ban be lifted in the event of a comprehensive nuclear deal.*

The harmonization of U.S. and European sanctions on Iran differs from early periods. During the 1990s, EU countries maintained a policy of "critical dialogue" with Iran, and the EU and Japan refused to join the 1995 U.S. trade and investment ban on Iran. The European dialogue with Iran was suspended in April 1997 in response to the German terrorism trial ("Mykonos trial") that found high-level Iranian involvement in killing Iranian dissidents in Germany, but resumed in May 1998 during Mohammad Khatemi's presidency of Iran. In the 1990s, European and Japanese creditors bucked U.S. objections and rescheduled about $16 billion in Iranian debt bilaterally, in spite of Paris Club rules that call for multilateral rescheduling. In July 2002, Iran tapped international capital markets for the first time since the Islamic revolution, selling $500 million in

---

[32] Avi Jorish, "Despite Sanctions, Iran's Money Flow Continues," *Wall Street Journal*, June 25, 2013.

bonds to European banks. During 2002-2005, there were active negotiations between the European Union and Iran on a "Trade and Cooperation Agreement" (TCA) that would have lowered the tariffs or increased quotas for Iranian exports to the EU countries.[33] Negotiations were discontinued in late 2005 after Iran abrogated an agreement to suspend uranium enrichment. Similarly, there has, to date, been insufficient international support to grant Iran membership in the World Trade Organization (WTO), even though U.S. Administrations ceased blocking Iran from applying in May 2005.

Japan and Korean Peninsula

In 2010, in part out of obligation to their alliance with the United States, Japan and South Korea imposed trade, banking, and energy Iran sanctions similar to those of the European Union. Both countries have cut imports of Iranian oil sharply since 2011. Some South Korean firms have been active in energy infrastructure construction in Iran but, on December 16, 2011, South Korea banned sales to Iran of energy sector equipment. The main South Korean refiners that import Iranian crude are SK Energy and Hyundai Oilbank.

The U.S. sanctions that require on oil buyers pay Iran in local accounts to avoid U.S. sanctions—a requirement that took effect on February 6, 2013—have not affected Japan and South Korea's trading patterns with Iran significantly. South Korea pays Iran's Central Bank through local currency accounts at its Industrial Bank of Korea and Woori Bank, and its main exports to Iran have been iron and steel, as well as consumer electronics and appliances made by companies such as Samsung and LG. Japan exports to Iran significant amounts of chemical and rubber products, as well as consumer electronics. These exports are continuing using local currency accounts. The two countries have been the source of the direct hard currency payments to Iran for oil under the JPA (a total of $4.2 billion in such direct payments is allowed during the JPA period).

North Korea

North Korea is an ally of Iran and, like Iran, is a subject of international sanctions. North Korea generally does not comply with international sanctions against Iran, and reportedly cooperates with Iran on a wide range of WMD-related ventures. Press reports in April 2013 said that Iran might supply oil directly to North Korea, but it has not been reported that any such arrangement was finalized. Currently, according to experts, a portion of China's purchases of oil from Iran and other suppliers is re-exported to North Korea.

India

India has implemented U.N.-mandated sanctions against Iran but its cultural, economic, and historic ties to Iran—as well as its strategic need for access to Afghanistan—have made the Indian government hesitant to impose all the sanctions on Iran that the United States and the EU have imposed. Yet, India's private sector increasingly has viewed Iran as a "controversial market"—a term used by many international firms to describe markets that entail significant reputational and financial risks.

---

[33] During the active period of talks, which began in December 2002, there were working groups focused not only on the TCA terms and proliferation issues but also on Iran's human rights record, Iran's efforts to derail the Middle East peace process, Iranian-sponsored terrorism, counter-narcotics, refugees, migration issues, and the Iranian opposition PMOI.

India began reducing economic relations with Iran in 2010, when India's central bank ceased using a Tehran-based regional body, the Asian Clearing Union, to handle transactions with Iran. In January 2012, Iran agreed to accept India's local currency, the rupee, to settle 45% of its sales to India. That local account funds the sale to Iran of Indian wheat, pharmaceuticals, rice, sugar, soybeans, auto parts, and other products. Still, there is a large trade imbalance, because the oil Iran exports to India are worth far more than the value of the products that India sells to an.

Even though purchases of Iranian oil are financially advantageous because of the barter nature of their trade, India has reduced its imports of Iranian oil substantially since 2011 in an effort to conform to U.S. and EU policy. By the end of 2012, Iran was only supplying about 10% of India's oil imports (down from over 16% in 2008). That percentage declined further to about 6% by mid-2013, despite the need for significant investment to switch over refineries that handle Iranian crude. During a visit to India on June 24, 2013, Secretary of State John Kerry praised India's Iranian oil import cuts as an "important step" in bringing pressure on Iran over its nuclear program. India has received and maintained an exemption from Section 1245 (P.L. 112-81) sanctions, as discussed. As shown in the table later in this report, some Indian firms have ended their investment activity in Iranian oil and gas fields since 2012.

India's weak economy in 2014 could cause U.S.-India differences on Iran sanctions. In mid-August 2013, India's finance minister said that India wants to increase oil imports from Iran.[34] Because Indian firms can pay for Iranian oil partly with rupees, buying Iranian oil helps India conserve its supply of dollars. India reportedly increased shipments from Iran during January-March 2014 to about 320,000 bpd, but U.S. officials say India plans to make cuts during April-June 2014 to bring average purchases in line with the pre-JPA level of about 200,000 bpd.

In 2009, India dissociated itself from an Iran-Pakistan gas pipeline project, discussed below, over concerns about the security of the pipeline, the location at which the gas would be transferred to India, pricing of the gas, and tariffs. During economic talks in early July 2010, Iranian and Indian officials reportedly raised the issue of constructing an underwater natural gas pipeline, which would avoid going through Pakistani territory. However, such a route would be much more expensive to construct than would be an overland route.

Pakistan

A test of Pakistan's compliance with sanctions is a pipeline project intended to carry Iranian gas to Pakistan. Agreement on the $7 billion project was finalized on June 12, 2010, and construction was formally inaugurated in a ceremony attended by the Presidents of both countries on March 11, 2013. With a formally agreed completion date of mid-2014, Iran reportedly has completed the pipeline on its side of the border. Potentially complicating the construction on the Pakistani side of the border is that Pakistan has had difficulty arranging about $1 billion in financing for the project. The day of the ceremony, the State Department reiterated comments during the Bush and Obama Administrations that the project might be sanctioned under ISA. In March 2014, possibly in part because of a Saudi grant to Pakistan that might have been intended to persuade Pakistan to distance itself from Iran, Pakistani officials said U.S. sanctions precluded construction on the

---

[34] Prasanta Sahu and Biman Mukherji, "New Delhi Looks to Buy More Iran Oil, Risks U.S. Ire," *Wall Street Journal*, August 13, 2013. p. 8.

Pakistan side of the border.[35] Still, Pakistan is obligated to begin buying gas from Iran as of January 1, 2015, lest it incur a $200 million per month penalty due Iran.

China and Russia

The position of Russia and China, two permanent members of the U.N. Security Council, is that they will impose only those sanctions required by U.N. Security Council resolutions. Russia has earned hard currency from large projects in Iran, such as the Bushehr nuclear reactor, and it also seeks not to provoke Iran into supporting Islamist movements in the Muslim regions of Russia and the Central Asian states. Press reports in mid-2014 indicate that Russia and Iran might be close to finalizing an agreement under which they would barter Iranian oil (500,000 barrels per day) for Russian goods. That deal would appear to violate the JPA.[36] Russia is an oil exporter and a need to preserve oil imports from Iran has not been a factor in its Iran policy calculations. The Iranian oil that Russia might buy under this arrangement, were it to be finalized, would presumably free up additional Russian oil for export.

China has been of concern to U.S. officials because it is Iran's largest oil customer, and therefore its cooperation has been pivotal to U.S. efforts to reduce Iran's revenue from oil sales. U.S.-China negotiations in mid-2012 led to an agreement for China to cut Iranian oil purchases by about 18% from its 2011 average of about 550,000 barrels per day to about 450,000 barrels per day. Under Secretary of State Wendy Sherman and Under Secretary of the Treasury David Cohen testified before the House Foreign Affairs Committee and Senate Foreign Relations Committee on May 15, 2013, that China had cut its buys of oil from Iran by 21% from 2011 to 2012 (to about 435,000 barrels per day). Iran's overall oil exports have fallen slightly further since, as shown in the table. As is the case with other Iranian oil customers, some months might show spikes to higher levels as oil shipments get scheduled. Because China is the largest buyer of Iranian oil, percentage cuts by China have a large impact in reducing Iran's oil sales by volume—explaining China's maintenance of its Section 1245 U.S. sanctions exemption. Several Chinese energy firms invested in Iran's energy sector, but some of these projects have been given to Iranian or other country firms after the Chinese investing firms failed to begin actual development work.

A February 6, 2013, U.S. sanction requiring that Iran be paid in local currency accounts caused Iran to further increase importation from China. Even before that sanction was imposed, China had begun to settle much of its trade balance with Iran with goods rather than hard currency. Doing so was highly favorable to China financially. Some reports in August 2013 indicated that China might settle some of its Iran oil bill by providing 315 subway cars for the Tehran metro.[37] Press reports indicated that Iran's automotive sector obtains a significant proportion of its parts from China, and two Chinese companies, Geelran and Chery, produce cars in Iran. These exports were reduced substantially during 2013 because of U.S. sanctions, but recovered somewhat after the JPA took effect, which requires easing sanctions on Iran's automotive sector.

---

[35] Asia Times, March 21, 2014. http://www.atimes.com/atimes/South_Asia/SOU-02-210314.html.

[36] "Iran, Russia Negotiating Big Oil-for-Goods Deal." Reuters, January 10, 2014.

[37] Author conversation with journalists based in China, September 1, 2013.

Turkey/South Caucasus

The relationship between Turkey and Iran deteriorated after 2011 as both took opposite sides on the Syria civil conflict. However, Turkey remains a significant buyer of Iranian oil; in 2011, it averaged nearly 200,000 bpd. Turkey subsequently reduced those purchases and Turkey received a Section 1245 NDAA sanctions exemption on June 11, 2012, renewed every six months thereafter. Some press reports have accused Turkey's Halkbank of settling much of Turkey's payments to Iran for oil or natural gas with shipments to Iran of gold. U.S. officials testified on May 15, 2013, that Turkey is not paying for its gas imports from Iran with gold, but that the gold going from Turkey to Iran consists mainly of Iranian private citizens' purchases of Turkish gold to hedge against the value of the *rial*. In line with cuts in Turkey's purchases of Iranian oil, overall bilateral trade fell to $15 billion in 2013 from $22 billion in 2012. On June 9, 2014, Rouhani visited Ankara, accompanied by more than 100 Iranian businessmen, and the two vowed to double bilateral trade to $30 billion by 2015.

Turkey buys natural gas from Iran via a pipeline built in 1997. Turkey is Iran's main gas customer because Iran has not developed a liquefied natural gas (LNG) export capability. During the pipeline's construction, the State Department testified that Turkey would be importing gas originating in Turkmenistan, not Iran, under a swap arrangement, and the State Department did not determine that the project was a violation of ISA. In 2001, direct Iranian gas exports to Turkey through the line began, but no ISA sanctions were imposed. Many experts assert that the State Department views the line as crucial to the energy security of Turkey, which is a key U.S. ally. Prior to the EU decision on October 15, 2012, to bar sales of Iranian gas to Europe, Turkey was also the main conduit for Iranian gas exports to Europe (primarily Bulgaria and Greece). Turkey said in December 2012 that it is constructing a second Iran-Turkey gas pipeline (the work is being performed by Som Petrol). No determination of sanctions violation has been announced.[38]

On January 6, 2014, the Commerce Department issued an emergency order blocking a Turkey-based firm (3K Aviation Consulting and Logistics) from re-exporting two U.S.-made jet engines to Iran. That and other firms reportedly involved in the deal denied that the engines were bound for an Iranian airline (Pouya Airline).[39]

Caucasus: Azerbaijan, Armenia, and Georgia

The Clinton and George W. Bush Administrations used the threat of ISA sanctions to deter oil pipeline routes involving Iran and thereby successfully promoted an alternate route from Azerbaijan (Baku) to Turkey (Ceyhan). The route became operational in 2005. Section 6 of Executive Order 13622 exempts from sanctions under Section 5 of the Order any pipelines that bring gas from Azerbaijan to Europe and Turkey.

In part because Iran and Azerbaijan are often at odds, Iran and Armenia—Azerbaijan's adversary—enjoy extensive economic relations. Armenia is Iran's largest direct gas customer, after Turkey. In May 2009, Iran and Armenia inaugurated a natural gas pipeline between the two, built by Gazprom of Russia. No determination of sanctionability has been announced. Armenia

[38] Information provided to the author by the New York State government, July 2012.
[39] "US Acts to Block Turkish Firm from Sending GE Engines to Iran." Reuters, January 6, 2014.

has said its banking controls are strong and that Iran is unable to process transactions illicitly through Armenia's banks.[40] However, Azerbaijani officials assert that Iran is using Armenian banks operating in the Armenia-occupied Nagorno-Karabakh territory to circumvent international financial sanctions. These institutions could include Artsakhbank and Ameriabank.[41] In May 2014, Iran and Armenia increased weekly flights between the two from 3 to 50, suggesting that commerce between the two is growing.

Some press reports say that Iran might have used another Caucasian state, Georgia, to circumvent sanctions. IRGC companies reportedly have established 150 front companies in Georgia for the purpose of importing dual-use items, but also to boost Iran's non-oil exports with sales to Georgia of Iranian products such as roofing materials and jams. Iranian firms reportedly are investing in Georgian companies and buying Georgian land.[42] On the other hand, observers assert that since extensive Iran-Georgia economic ties were highly publicized in mid-2013, Georgia has sought and obtained cooperation from its businessmen in reducing transactions with Iran.

Persian Gulf and Iraq[43]

The Persian Gulf countries are oil exporters and close allies of the United States. Those Gulf states with spare oil production capacity, particularly Saudi Arabia, have supplied the global oil market with extra oil to keep prices steady in the face of reduced Iranian oil exports. The Gulf states have generally sought to prevent the re-exportation to Iran of U.S. technology, and have curtailed banking relationships with Iran. On the other hand, in order not to antagonize Iran, the Gulf countries still conduct a wide range of trade with Iran and some Gulf countries allow some sanctioned Iranian banks to operating in their countries. Gulf-based shipping companies such as United Arab Shipping Company have continued to pay port loading fees to such sanctioned IRGC-controlled port operators as Tidewater.[44]

The UAE is particularly closely watched by U.S. officials because of the large presence of Iranian firms there. Several UAE-based firms have been sanctioned for efforts to evade sanctions, as noted in the tables at the end of the report. U.S. officials praised the UAE's March 1, 2012, ban on transactions with Iran by Dubai-based Noor Islamic Bank. Iran reportedly used the bank to process a substantial portion of its oil payments. Some Iranian gas condensate (120,000 barrels per day) reportedly has been imported by Emirates National Oil Company (ENOC) and refined into jet fuel, gasoline, and other products.

Iran and Kuwait have held talks on the construction of a 350-mile pipeline that would bring Iranian gas to Kuwait. No construction has been reported. The two have apparently reached agreement on volumes (8.5 million cubic meters of gas would go to Kuwait each day) but not on price.[45] Kuwait's Amir visited Iran in early June 2014.

---

[40] Louis Charbonneau, "Iran Looks to Armenia to Skirt Banking Sanctions," *Reuters*, August 21, 2012.

[41] Information provided to the author by regional observers. October 2013.

[42] "As Sanctions Bite, Iran Invests Big in Georgia," *Wall Street Journal*, June 20, 2013.

[43] The CRS Report RL32048, *Iran: U.S. Concerns and Policy Responses*, by Kenneth Katzman, discusses the relations between Iran and other Middle Eastern states.

[44] Mark Wallace, "Closing U.S. Ports to Iran-Tainted Shipping. Op-ed," *Wall Street Journal*, March 15, 2013.

[45] http://www.kuwaittimes.net/read_news.php?newsid=NDQ0OTY1NTU4; http://english.farsnews.com/newstext.php?nn=8901181055.

Iran has sought to use its close relations with Iraq to evade some sanctions. As noted above, the United States sanctioned an Iraqi bank that has cooperated with Iran's efforts, but lifted those sanctions when the bank reduced that business. Iraq presented the United States with a more significant Iran sanctions-related dilemma on July 23, 2013, when it signed an agreement with Iran to buy 850 million cubic feet per day of natural gas through a joint pipeline that reportedly is nearing construction. The pipeline will enter Iraq at Diyala province and feed several power plants. The two countries signed a contract for the pipeline construction in July 2011, and it reportedly is close to completion on both sides of the border; its construction costs are estimated at about $365 million.[46]

The United States has also has pressed Iraq, with limited success, to inspect flights from Iran to Syria to enforce cooperation with U.N. sanctions that ban Iran from exporting arms. However, the Iraq crisis that began in June 2014 has prompted further apparent U.N. sanctions violations by Iran. Iran has shipped tons of military equipment and supplies to the beleaguered Iraq Security Forces to help them defend against the offensive by the Islamic State.[47]

Afghanistan

Some reports say that Iranian currency traders are using Afghanistan to acquire dollars that are plentiful there but in short supply in Iran. Iranian traders—acting on behalf of wealthy Iranians seeking to preserve the value of their savings—are said to be carrying local currency to Afghanistan to buy up some of the dollars available there. There are also allegations that Iran is using an Iran-owned bank in Afghanistan, Arian Bank, to move funds in and out of Afghanistan. The U.S. Treasury Department has warned Afghan traders not to process dollar transactions for Iran. The Special Inspector General for Afghanistan Reconstruction reported in late January 2013 that Afghan security forces might have used some of U.S. aid funds to purchase fuel from Iran. In September 2013, it was reported that Anham FZCO, a U.S. contractor building food storage shelters for U.S. troops in Afghanistan, might have violated U.S. sanctions by transshipping building materials through Iran.[48]

Latin America

Iran, during the term of President Ahmadinejad, looked to several Latin American countries, particularly Venezuela, to try to avoid or reduce the effects of international sanctions. For the most part, however, Iran's trade and other business dealings with Latin America remain modest and likely to reduce the effect of sanctions on Iran only marginally. And, Iran lost a key Latin American ally with the March 2013 death of Venezuelan President Hugo Chavez. As noted elsewhere in this report, several Venezuelan firms have been sanctioned for dealings with Iran.

---

[46] Ben Lando, "Iraq Inks Gas Supply Deal with Iran," *Iraq Oil Report*, July 23, 2013.

[47] Michael Gordon and Eric Schmitt. "Iran Secretly Sending Drones and Supplies to Iraq, U.S. Officials Say." New York Times, June 25, 2014.

[48] "Pentagon Contractor Used Iran for Project," *Wall Street Journal*, September 26, 2013.

Africa

During the term of Ahmadinejad, Iran sought to cultivate relations with some African countries to try to circumvent sanctions. However, African countries have tended to avoid dealings with Iran in order to avoid pressure from the United States. South Africa has ended its buys of Iranian oil. In June 2012, Kenya contracted to buy about 30 million barrels of Iranian oil, but cancelled the contract the following month after the United States warned that going ahead with the purchase could hurt U.S.-Kenya relations. In June 2012, then-Representative Howard Berman sent a letter to Tanzania's president warning that Tanzania could face aid cuts or other punishments if it continued to "re-flag" Iranian oil tankers.[49] Tanzania has re-flagged about 6-10 Iranian tankers. Perhaps fearing similar criticism, in September 2012 Sierra Leone removed nine vessels from its shipping register after determining they belonged to IRISL.

World Bank Loans

The July 27, 2010, EU measures narrowed substantially the prior differences between the EU and the United States over international lending to Iran. As noted above, the United States representative to international financial institutions is required to vote against international lending, but that vote, although weighted, is not sufficient to block international lending. No new loans have been approved to Iran since 2005, including several environmental projects under the Bank's "Global Environmental Facility" (GEF). The initiative has slated more than $7.5 million in loans for Iran to dispose of harmful chemicals.[50]

Earlier, in 1993, the United States voted its 16.5% share of the World Bank against loans to Iran of $460 million for electricity, health, and irrigation projects, but the loans were approved. To block that lending, the FY1994-FY1996 foreign aid appropriations (P.L. 103-87, P.L. 103-306, and P.L. 104-107) cut the amount appropriated for the U.S. contribution to the bank by the amount of those loans. The legislation contributed to a temporary halt in new bank lending to Iran. In the 111th Congress, a provision of H.R. 6296—Title VII—cut off U.S. contributions to the World Bank, International Finance Corp., and the Multilateral Investment Guarantee Corp. if the World Bank approves a new Country Assistance Strategy for Iran or makes a loan to Iran.

During 1999-2005, Iran's moderating image had led the World Bank to consider new loans over U.S. opposition. In May 2000, the United States' allies outvoted the United States to approve $232 million in loans for health and sewage projects. During April 2003-May 2005, a total of $725 million in loans were approved for environmental management, housing reform, water and sanitation projects, and land management projects, in addition to $400 million in loans for earthquake relief.

---

[49] "Tanzania Must Stop Re-Flagging Iran Tankers: U.S. Lawmaker," *Reuters*, June 29, 2012.

[50] Barbara Slavin. "Obama Administration Holds Up Environmental Grants to Iran." Al Monitor, June 23, 2014.

Table 4. Comparison Between U.S., U.N., and EU and Allied Country Sanctions

U.S. Sanctions	U.N. Sanctions	Implementation by EU and Some Allied Countries
General Observation: Most sweeping sanctions on Iran of virtually any country in the world	Increasingly sweeping, but still intended to primarily target Iran's nuclear and other WMD programs. No mandatory sanctions on Iran's energy sector.	EU abides closely aligns its sanctions tightening—as well as sanctions relief in the context of the nuclear deal—with those of the U.S. Japan and South Korean sanctions also increasingly extensive.
Ban on U.S. Trade with and Investment in Iran: Executive Order 12959 bans (with limited exceptions) U.S. firms from exporting to Iran, importing from Iran, or investing in Iran. There is an exemption for sales to Iran of food and medical products.	U.N. sanctions do not ban civilian trade with Iran or general civilian sector investment in Iran. Nor do U.N. sanctions mandate restrictions on provision of trade financing or financing guarantees by national export credit guarantee agencies.	No general EU ban on trade in civilian goods with Iran, but bans on certain types of trade as discussed. Japan and South Korea have banned medium- and long-term trade financing and financing guarantees. Short-term credit still allowed.
Sanctions on Foreign Firms that Do Business with Iran's Energy Sector: The Iran Sanctions Act, P.L. 104-172, and subsequent laws and executive orders, discussed throughout the report, mandate sanctions on virtually any type of transaction with/in Iran's energy sector. Some exemptions are permitted for firms of countries that have "significantly reduced" purchases of Iranian oil each 180 days.	No U.N. equivalent exists. However, preambular language in Resolution 1929 "not[es] the potential connection between Iran's revenues derived from its energy sector and the funding of Iran's proliferation-sensitive nuclear activities." This wording is interpreted by most observers as providing U.N. support for countries who want to ban their companies from investing in Iran's energy sector.	With certain exceptions likely to fulfill the nuclear deal, the EU bans almost all dealings with Iran's energy sector. Japanese and South Korean measures ban new energy projects in Iran and call for restraint on ongoing projects. South Korea in December 2011 cautioned its firms not to sell energy or petrochemical equipment to Iran. Both have cut oil purchases from Iran sharply.
Ban on Foreign Assistance: U.S. foreign assistance to Iran—other than purely humanitarian aid—is banned under §620A of the Foreign Assistance Act, which bans U.S. assistance to countries on the U.S. list of "state sponsors of terrorism." Iran is also routinely denied direct U.S. foreign aid under the annual foreign operations appropriations acts (most recently in §7007 of division H of P.L. 111-8).	No U.N. equivalent	EU measures of July 27, 2010, ban grants, aid, and concessional loans to Iran. Also prohibit financing of enterprises involved in Iran's energy sector. Japan and South Korea measures do not specifically ban aid or lending to Iran, but no such lending by these countries is under way.
Ban on Arms Exports to Iran: Iran is ineligible for U.S. arms exports under several laws, as discussed in the report.	Resolution 1929 (operative paragraph 8) bans all U.N. member states from selling or supplying to Iran major weapons systems, including tanks, armored vehicles, combat aircraft, warships, and most missile systems, or related spare parts or advisory services for such weapons systems.	EU sanctions include a comprehensive ban on sale to Iran of all types of military equipment, not just major combat systems. No similar Japan and South Korean measures announced, but neither has exported arms to Iran.

U.S. Sanctions	U.N. Sanctions	Implementation by EU and Some Allied Countries
Restriction on Exports to Iran of "Dual Use Items": Primarily under §6(j) of the Export Administration Act (P.L. 96-72) and §38 of the Arms Export Control Act, there is a denial of license applications to sell Iran goods that could have military applications.	The U.N. resolutions on Iran, cumulatively, ban the export of almost all dual-use items to Iran.	EU bans the sales of dual use items to Iran, in line with U.N. resolutions. Japan and S. Korea have announced full adherence to strict export control regimes when evaluating sales to Iran.
Sanctions Against International Lending to Iran: Under §1621 of the International Financial Institutions Act (P.L. 95-118), U.S. representatives to international financial institutions, such as the World Bank, are required to vote against loans to Iran by those institutions.	Resolution 1747 (oper. paragraph 7) requests, but does not mandate, that countries and international financial institutions refrain from making grants or loans to Iran, except for development and humanitarian purposes.	The July 27, 2010, measures prohibit EU members from providing grants, aid, and concessional loans to Iran, including through international financial institutions. No specific similar Japan or South Korea measures announced.
Sanctions Against Foreign Firms that Sell Weapons of Mass Destruction-Related Technology to Iran: As discussed in this report, several laws and regulations provide for sanctions against entities, Iranian or otherwise, that are determined to be involved in or supplying Iran's WMD programs (asset freezing, ban on transaction with the entity).	Resolution 1737 (oper. paragraph 12) imposes a worldwide freeze on the assets and property of Iranian entities named in an Annex to the Resolution. Each subsequent resolution has expanded the list of Iranian entities subject to these sanctions.	The EU measures imposed July 27, 2010, commit the EU to freezing the assets of entities named in the U.N. resolutions, as well as numerous other named Iranian entities. Japan and South Korea froze assets of U.N.-sanctioned entities.
Ban on Transactions with Terrorism Supporting Entities: Executive Order 13224 bans transactions with entities determined by the Administration to be supporting international terrorism. Numerous entities, including some of Iranian origin, have been so designated.	No direct equivalent, but Resolution 1747 (oper. paragraph 5) bans Iran from exporting any arms—a provision widely interpreted as trying to reduce Iran's material support to groups such as Lebanese Hezbollah, Hamas, Shiite militias in Iraq, and insurgents in Afghanistan.	No direct equivalent, but many of the Iranian entities named as blocked by the EU, Japan, and South Korea overlap or complement Iranian entities named as terrorism supporting by the United States.
Travel Ban on Named Iranians: CISADA and H.R. 1905 provide for a prohibition on travel to the U.S., blocking of U.S.-based property, and ban on transactions with Iranians determined to be involved in serious human rights abuses against Iranians since the June 12, 2009, presidential election there, or with persons selling Iran equipment to commit such abuses.	Resolution 1803 imposed a binding ban on international travel by several Iranians named in an Annex to the Resolution. Resolution 1929 extended that ban to additional Iranians, and forty Iranians are now subject to the ban. However, the Iranians subject to the travel ban are so subjected because of their involvement in Iran's WMD programs, not because of involvement in human rights abuses.	The EU sanctions announced July 27, 2010, contains an Annex of named Iranians subject to a ban on travel to the EU countries. An additional 60+ Iranians involved in human rights abuses were subjected to EU sanctions since. Japan and South Korea have announced bans on named Iranians.

U.S. Sanctions	U.N. Sanctions	Implementation by EU and Some Allied Countries
Restrictions on Iranian Shipping: Under Executive Order 13382, the U.S. Treasury Department has named Islamic Republic of Iran Shipping Lines and several affiliated entities as entities whose U.S.-based property is to be frozen.	Resolution 1803 and 1929 authorize countries to inspect cargoes carried by Iran Air and Islamic Republic of Iran Shipping Lines (IRISL)—or any ships in national or international waters—if there is an indication that the shipments include goods whose export to Iran is banned.	The EU measures announced July 27, 2010, bans Iran Air Cargo from access to EU airports. The measures also freeze the EU-based assets of IRISL and its affiliates. Insurance and re-insurance for Iranian firms is banned. Japan and South Korean measures took similar actions against IRISL and Iran Air.
Banking Sanctions: During 2006-2011, several Iranian banks have been named as proliferation or terrorism supporting entities under Executive Orders 13382 and 13224, respectively (see **Table 5** at end of report). CISADA prohibits banking relationships with U.S. banks for any foreign bank that conducts transactions with Iran's Revolutionary Guard or with Iranian entities sanctioned under the various U.N. resolutions. FY2012 Defense Authorization (P.L. 112-81) prevents U.S. accounts with foreign banks that process transactions with Iran's Central Bank (with specified exemptions).	No direct equivalent However, two Iranian banks are named as sanctioned entities under the U.N. Security Council resolutions.	The EU froze Iran Central Bank assets January 23, 2012, and banned all transactions with Iranian banks unless authorized on October 15, 2012. Brussels-based SWIFT expelled sanctioned Iranian banks from the electronic payment transfer system. Japan and South Korea measures similar to the 2010 EU sanctions, with South Korea adhering to the same 40,000 Euro authorization requirement. Japan and S. Korea froze the assets of 15 Iranian banks; South Korea targeted Bank Mellat for freeze. Some measures by these allies likely to be eased to implement nuclear deal.
No direct equivalent, although, as discussed above, U.S. proliferations laws provide for sanctions against foreign entities that help Iran with its nuclear and ballistic missile programs.	Resolution 1929 (oper. paragraph 7) prohibits Iran from acquiring an interest in any country involving uranium mining, production, or use of nuclear materials, or technology related to nuclear-capable ballistic missiles. Paragraph 9 prohibits Iran from undertaking "any activity" related to ballistic missiles capable of delivering a nuclear weapon.	EU measures on July 27, 2010, require adherence to this provision of Resolution 1929.

Private-Sector Cooperation and Compliance

The multiplicity of sanctions have caused Iran to be viewed by many worldwide corporations as a "controversial market"—a market that carries political and reputational risks even if some business in that market is not sanctionable. On the other hand, travelers to Iran say many foreign products, including U.S. products, are readily available in Iran, suggesting that such products are being re-exported to Iran from neighboring countries. Examples of major non-U.S. companies that, prior to the JPA, had discontinued business with Iran include the following:

- ABB of Switzerland said in January 2010 it would cease doing business with Iran. Siemens of Germany followed suit in February 2010. Finemeccanica, a defense and transportation conglomerate of Italy, and Thyssen-Krupp, a German steelmaker, subsequently left the Iran market as well. Indian conglomerate Tata is ending its Iran business.

- Auto manufacturing and sales of automotive equipment to Iran are sanctionable under Executive Order 13645. Sales of finished autos were not sanctionable, yet several firms ceased selling cars to Iran in 2010, including Germany's Daimler (Mercedes-Benz) and Porsche; Toyota (Japan); Fiat (Italy); and South Korea's Hyundai, and Kia Motors. French carmaker Peugeot, which produces cars locally in partnership with Iran's Khodro Group, suspended operations in Iran after E.O. 13645 took effect in July 2012. Peugeot is 7% owned by General Motors, but GM is not known to have any involvement in or to supply any GM content to the Peugeot Iran activities.

- Attorneys for BNP Paribas of France told the author in July 2011 that, as of 2007, the firm was pursuing no new business in Iran.

- The State Department reported on September 30, 2010, that Hong Kong company NYK Line Ltd. had ended shipping business with Iran on any goods. On June 30, 2011, the Danish shipping giant Maersk said that it would no longer operate out of Iran's three largest ports. The firm's decision reportedly was based on the U.S. announcement on June 23, 2011, of sanctions on the operator of those ports, Tidewater Middle East Co., under Executive Order 13382.

- Well before Executive Order 13590 was issued (see above), one large oil services firm, Schlumberger, incorporated in the Netherlands Antilles, said it would wind down its business with Iran.[51]

Foreign Subsidiaries of U.S. Firms That Have Exited the Iran Market

Even before their activities became sanctionable as a consequence of post-2010 legislation and executive orders, many foreign subsidiaries of U.S. firms had exited the Iran market voluntarily.

- Chemical manufacturer Huntsman announced in January 2010 its subsidiaries would halt sales to Iran.

- On January 11, 2005, Iran said it had contracted with U.S. company Halliburton, and an Iranian company, Oriental Kish, to drill for gas in Phases 9 and 10 of South Pars. Halliburton reportedly provided $30 million to $35 million worth of services per year through Oriental Kish, leaving unclear whether Halliburton would be considered in violation of the U.S. trade and investment ban or the Iran Sanctions Act (ISA),[52] because the deals involved a subsidiary of Halliburton (Cayman Islands-registered Halliburton Products and Service, Ltd., based in Dubai). On April 10, 2007, Halliburton announced that its subsidiaries were no longer operating in Iran, as promised in January 2005.

---

[51] Farah Stockman, "Oil Firm Says It Will Withdraw From Iran," *Boston Globe*, November 12, 2010.

[52] "Iran Says Halliburton Won Drilling Contract," *Washington Times*, January 11, 2005.

- General Electric (GE) announced in February 2005 that it would seek no new business in Iran, and it reportedly wound down preexisting contracts by July 2008. GE was selling Iran equipment and services for hydroelectric, oil, and gas services. However, GE subsidiary sales of medical diagnostic products such as MRI machines, sold through Italian, Canadian, and French subsidiaries, are not generally sanctionable and are believed to be continuing.

- On March 1, 2010, Caterpillar Corp. said it had altered its policies to prevent foreign subsidiaries from selling equipment to independent dealers that have been reselling the equipment to Iran.[53] Ingersoll Rand, maker of air compressors and cooling systems, followed suit.[54]

- In April 2010, it was reported that foreign partners of several U.S. or other multinational accounting firms had cut their ties with Iran, including KPMG of the Netherlands, and local affiliates of U.S. firms PricewaterhouseCoopers and Ernst and Young.[55]

- Oilfield services firm Smith International said on March 1, 2010, it would stop sales to Iran by its subsidiaries. Another oil services firm, Flowserve, said its subsidiaries have voluntarily ceased new business with Iran as of 2006.[56] FMC Technologies took similar action in 2009, as did Weatherford[57] in 2008. However, in November 2013, Weatherford was fined by the Treasury Department for violating sanctions against Iran and other countries.

Foreign Firms Reportedly Remaining in the Iran Market

Still, many major firms continue to run the financial risk of doing business with Iran. They include most of the major consumer products companies of Europe and Asia. Some of the foreign firms that trade with Iran, such as Mitsui and Co. of Japan, Alstom of France, and Schneider Electric of France, are discussed in a March 7, 2010, *New York Times* article on foreign firms that do business with Iran and also receive U.S. contracts or financing. The *Times* article does not claim that these firms have violated any U.S. sanctions laws. Internet and communications-related foreign firms remaining in or having departed the Iranian market are discussed in the section below on human rights effects of sanctions.

Some foreign firms still active in Iran are subsidiaries of U.S. firms and some of them also received U.S. government contracts, grants, loans, or loan guarantees. They include:

- An Irish subsidiary of the Coca Cola Company, which provides syrup for the U.S.-brand soft drink to an Iranian distributor, Khoshgovar. Local versions of both Coke and of Pepsi (with Iranian-made syrups) are also marketed in Iran by

---

[53] "Caterpillar Says Tightens 'No-Iran' Business Policy," *Reuters*, March 1, 2010.

[54] Ron Nixon, "2 Corporations Say Business With Tehran Will Be Curbed," *New York Times*, March 11, 2010.

[55] Peter Baker, "U.S. and Foreign Companies Feeling Pressure to Sever Ties With Iran," *New York Times*, April 24, 2010.

[56] In September 2011, the Commerce Department fined Flowserve $2.5 million to settle 288 charges of unlicensed exports and reexports of oil industry equipment to Iran, Syria, and other countries.

[57] Form 10-K for Fiscal year ended December 31, 2008, claims firm directed its subsidiaries to cease new business in Iran and Cuba, Syria, and Sudan as of September 2007.

distributors who licensed the recipes for those soft drinks before the Islamic revolution and before the trade ban was imposed on Iran.

- Via a Swiss-based subsidiary, Transammonia Corp. conducts business with Iran to help it export ammonia, a growth export for Iran.

- Kansas-based Koch Industries may have sold equipment to Iran to be used in petrochemical plants (making methanol) and possibly oil refineries, until 2007. Sales of refinery equipment to Iran were later made sanctionable under ISA.[58]

- Some subsidiaries of U.S. energy equipment and energy-related shipping firms were in the Iranian market as late as 2010, including Natco Group,[59] Overseas Shipholding Group,[60] UOP (United Oil Products, a Honeywell subsidiary based in Britain),[61] Itron,[62] Fluor,[63] Parker Drilling, Vantage Energy Services,[64] PMFG, Ceradyne, Colfax, Fuel Systems Solutions, General Maritime Company, Ameron International Corporation, and World Fuel Services Corp. UOP reportedly sold refinery gear to Iran. However, as of mid-2010 almost all energy sector-related sales to Iran are sanctionable and these companies have most likely exited the Iranian market.

Effectiveness of Sanctions on Iran

The following sections examine the effectiveness of sanctions on a variety of criteria and goals. These issues are discussed in depth in CRS Report R43492, *Achievements of and Outlook for Sanctions on Iran*, by Kenneth Katzman.

Effect on Iran's Nuclear Program Decisions and Capabilities

During the term of former President Mahmoud Ahmadinejad, U.S. and U.N. sanctions did not succeed in compelling Iran to verifiably limit its nuclear development to purely peaceful purposes. Many experts interpret Iran's acceptance of the JPA as evidence that sanctions contributed substantially to a shift in Iran's nuclear policies. The agreement came after the June 14, 2013, presidential election in Iran in which Iranians elected the relatively moderate mid-ranking cleric Hassan Rouhani as president; he ran on a platform of achieving an easing of sanctions and ending Iran's international isolation. However, Director of National Intelligence James Clapper testified in his "Worldwide Threat Assessment" presentation to Congress on

---

[58] Asjylyn Loder and David Evans, "Koch Brothers Flout Law Getting Richer With Iran Sales," *Bloomberg News*, October 3, 2011.

[59] Form 10-K Filed for fiscal year ended December 31, 2008.

[60] Paulo Prada and Betsy McKay, "Trading Outcry Intensifies," *Wall Street Journal*, March 27, 2007; Michael Brush, "Are You Investing in Terrorism?," *MSN Money*, July 9, 2007.

[61] *New York Times*, March 7, 2010, cited previously.

[62] "Subsidiaries of the Registrant at December 31, 2009," http://www.sec.gov/Archives/edgar/data/780571/000078057110000007/ex_21-1 htm.

[63] "Exhibit to 10-K Filed February 25, 2009." Officials of Fluor claim that their only dealings with Iran involve property in Iran owned by a Fluor subsidiary, which the subsidiary has been unable to dispose of. CRS conversation with Fluor, December 2009.

[64] Form 10-K for Fiscal year ended December 31, 2007.

January 29, 2014, that Iran's ultimate nuclear intentions remain "unclear." A comprehensive solution on Iran's nuclear program has been under negotiation between Iran and the "P5+1" countries (United States, Britain, France, Russia, China, and Germany) since February 2014 but did not reach agreement by the JPA expiration date of July 20, 2014. Based on reported progress in the negotiations, Iran and the P5+1 exercised the provision of the JPA to extend it for up to six months—opting for a four-month extension until November 24, 2014.

Effects on Iran's Strategic Programs and Regional Influence

A related issue is whether sanctions have weakened Iran strategically. One aspect of that question is whether sanctions have prevented Iran from acquiring needed technology or skills for its nuclear program or its missile or advanced conventional weapons programs. Sanctions did not prevent Iran from developing more advanced centrifuges and expanding its uranium enrichment program, as widely noted by the International Atomic Energy Agency (IAEA). Director of National Intelligence James Clapper has testified that Iran continues to expand the scale, reach, and sophistication of its ballistic missile arsenal. Some U.S. officials have asserted that sanctions have complicated Iran's efforts to acquire key materials and equipment for its enrichment program.[65] On the other hand, on March 16, 2014, Principal Deputy Assistant Secretary of State for International Security and Non-Proliferation Vann Van Diepen said Iran was still "very actively" creating front companies and engaging in other activity to conceal procurements, and that Iran's procurement activities had not changed since the JPA was agreed to.[66] See also CRS Report R40094, *Iran's Nuclear Program: Tehran's Compliance with International Obligations*, by Paul K. Kerr, and CRS Report R42849, *Iran's Ballistic Missile and Space Launch Programs*, by Steven A. Hildreth.

Sanctions might have eroded those aspects of Iran's conventional military capabilities that are most dependent on foreign supplies, but the effect of sanctions on Iran's overall military capacity is not clear. Resolution 1929 of June 2010 prohibited the sale to Iran of major combat systems, and there have been no reports of sales to Iran of tanks or combat aircraft since then. However, Iran might have acquired some ships and small submarines,[67] and Iran is able to produce some advanced conventional weaponry indigenously, including short range ballistic and cruise missiles.

Sanctions do not appear to have materially reduced Iran's ability to arm militant movements in the Middle East and the Syrian regime. As noted above, Iran reportedly is also exporting military equipment to the embattled government of Iraq in the wake of the Islamic State offensive in June 2014. Iran's arms exports contravene Resolution 1747, which bans Iran's exportation of arms.[68] The State Department report on international terrorism for 2013, released April 30, 2014, said Iran also has exported arms to factions in Yemen and to militant Palestinian Islamist factions, and has sought to supply arms to radical Shiite factions in Bahrain.

---

[65] Speech by National Security Adviser Tom Donilon at the Brookings Institution, November 22, 2011.

[66] William Maclean. "Iran Pursuing Banned Items for Nuclear, Missile Wor: U.S. Official." Reuters, March 16, 2014.

[67] Department of Defense, *Annual Report of Military Power of Iran*, April 2012.

[68] Louis Charbonneau, "U.N. Monitors See Arms Reaching Somalia From Yemen, Iran," *Reuters*, February 10, 2013.

General Political Effects

Sanctions might have produced some political change in Iran. Most of the candidates permitted by the regime to run for president in June 2013 were conservative allies of Khamene'i, but the support of Iranians seeking change powered the most moderate candidate in the race, Rouhani, to a first round victory. The Supreme Leader welcomed Rouhani's election and, because it achieves some sanctions relief, he has publicly backed the JPA and subsequent negotiations on a comprehensive solution.

No U.S. Administration has stated that sanctions on Iran are intended to bring about the change of Iran's regime. However, some Iran sanctions advocates have stated that outcome should be the goal of U.S. sanctions policy on Iran. The major unrest in Iran in 2009 was, by all accounts, a response to repression and alleged fraud in the June 2009 re-election of Mahmoud Ahmadinejad as president—and not linked to international sanctions. Since 2012 there have been labor and public unrest over escalating food prices and the dramatic fall of the value of Iran's currency. But the unrest has not been sufficiently large or sustained to threaten the regime.

Human Rights-Related Effects

Some see sanctions as a tool to compel improvement in human rights practices in Iran. The State Department human rights report for 2013, released February 27, 2014, contains many of the same criticisms of Iran's human rights practices as do the reports for previous years. That and other reports note that President Rouhani has released a few political prisoners and press reports say media freedoms have increased slightly since he took office. However, executions have, by some accounts, become more frequent. The connection between any of these trends and international sanctions is unclear.

Sanctions have not reduced the regime's ability to monitor and censor use of the Internet. However, some major firms that might have contributed to Iran's censorship and monitoring capabilities have exited the Iran market. Among those exiting are German telecommunications firm Siemens, which announced on January 27, 2010, that it would stop signing new business deals in Iran as of mid-2010.[69] Chinese Internet infrastructure firm Huawei announced in December 2011 that it was withdrawing its sales staff from Iran. A South African firm, MTN Group, owns 49% of a private cellular phone network, Irancell, and was accused by some groups of helping the Iranian government shut down some social network services during the 2009 protests in Iran.[70] On August 8, 2012, MTN announced it would leave Iran. On October 11, 2012, Eutelsat, a significant provider of satellite service to Iran's state broadcasting establishment, ended that relationship following EU sanctioning in March 2012 of the head of the Islamic Republic of Iran Broadcasting (IRIB) Ezzatollah Zarghami. The GAO report of January 7, 2014, did not identify any foreign firms that exported technology to Iran for monitoring, filtering, or disrupting information and communications flow from October 1, 2012, to November 7, 2013.[71]

---

[69] Aurelia End, "Siemens Quits Iran Amid Mounting Diplomatic Tensions," *Agence France Press*, January 27, 2010.

[70] http://www.examiner.com/article/obama-adviser-plouffe-received-100-000-from-iranian-associated-firm.

[71] GAO-14-218R Iran, January 7, 2014.

Some major telecommunications firms have remained in the Iran market, although it is not clear whether their products help either the regime or the opposition. They include Deutsche Telekom, Ericsson, Emirates Telecom, LG Group, NEC Corporation, and Asiasat.

Economic Effects

Many experts attribute Iran's acceptance of the JPA to the toll sanctions have taken on Iran's economy. The sanctions amplified the effect of Iran's own mismanagement, according to experts. Indicators of the economic effect of sanctions, as well as any beneficial effects of the JPA sanctions relief, are discussed below:

- *GDP Decline.* Sanctions caused Iran to suffer its first gross domestic product (GDP) contraction in two decades—it dropped about 5% in 2013. Under Secretary of the Treasury for Terrorism and Financial Intelligence David Cohen testified before the Senate Foreign Relations Committee on July 29, 2014, that Iran's economy is 25% smaller than it would have been had it remained on pre-2011 projections (before many of the most stringent sanctions were imposed). Many Iranian businesses failed, the number of non-performing loans increased, and many employees in the private sector went unpaid or were subject to long delays in payments. The unemployment rate rose to about 20%, although the Iranian government reported that the rate at 13%. The sanctions relief of the JPA has stabilized the economy somewhat—Iran's economy is expected to achieve slight growth of about 1%-1.5% for all of 2014, according to the International Monetary Fund. However, the sanctions relief has not been sufficient to produce a strong economic rebound. Treasury Secretary Jack Lew said on June 16, 2014, that "Iran's economy remains in a state of distress that brought the government to the negotiating table in the first place."[72]

- *Oil Exports.* As noted in **Table 2**, sanctions drove Iran's oil sales down about 60% from the 2.5 mbd of sales in 2011, reducing Iran's oil sales revenue from $100 billion in 2011 to about $35 billion in 2013. The JPA specifies that Iran's oil sales remain constant at *about* 1 mbd for the six-month duration of the deal. (State Department officials say that 1.1 mbd of exports would be within their interpretation of the JPA limit.)[73] International Energy Agency (IEA) and other data indicate that Iran's exports of crude oil are within that prescribed range. Deputy Assistant Secretary of State Amos Hochstein testified before the House Foreign Affairs Committee on June 11, 2014, that "So far [in JPA implementation], as we look at the [Iranian crude oil export] numbers, we are comfortable [that] at the moment, those numbers ... are kept to that range of 1 million to 1.1 million barrels a day." However, U.S. officials confirmed at the July 29, 2014, Senate Foreign Relations Committee hearing, referenced earlier, that Iran is also exporting oil to Syria gratis (not counted as a *sale*) and it is exporting condensates. Condensates are a petroleum product that is used to make plastics and, when exported from a natural gas field, purchases of condensates are not penalized by U.S. sanctions.[74] If these exports were counted as barrels of

---

[72] "Iran Economy Remains in Distress Amid Sanctions—U.S.'s Lew." Reuters, June 18, 2014.

[73] "Why Higher Iran Oil Exports Are Not Roiling Nuclear Deal." Reuters, June 13, 2014.

[74] Ibid.

oil per day, Iran would be exporting about 1.4 mbd,[75] although Iran receives no funds from Syria for the approximately 100,000 barrels per day Tehran sends there.

- *Falling Oil Production.* At the time the JPA began implementation, Iran's oil production had fallen to about 2.6-2.8 mbd from the level of nearly 4.0 mbd at the end of 2011.[76] Iran has tried to avoid further production cuts by storing as many as 30 million barrels of unsold crude oil on tankers in the Persian Gulf, and it built additional storage tanks on shore. U.S. officials say that production is holding steady at this lower level and that Iran has largely succeeded in preventing damage to shut or inactive wells.

- *Hard Currency Inaccessible.* Not only have Iran's oil exports fallen by volume, but Iran has not been paid in hard currency for its oil and is unable to access most of its hard currency held in accounts abroad. Prior to the implementation of the JPA, about $1.5 billion per month was accumulating in foreign accounts, out of about $3.4 billion in the total value of monthly oil sales[77]—in part because Iran cannot always identify a sufficient amount of goods in those countries to import to make use of all the oil money it receives. Iran's hard currency reserves are estimated to be nearly $100 billion, of which as much as $80 billion cannot be repatriated due to compliance by banks with U.S. sanctions. About $20 billion is believed to be accessible—aside from the $700 million per month Iran has received directly since the JPA became effective.

- *Currency Decline.* Sanctions caused the value of the rial on unofficial markets to decline from about 13,000 to the dollar in September 2011 to about 40,000 as of October 2012. The unofficial rate was about 37,000 to the dollar in May 2013, but optimism over Rouhani's presidency and the JPA caused the *rial* to appreciate to about 29,000 to the dollar as of the start of 2014 and to remain roughly at that level.

- *Inflation.* The drop in value of the currency caused inflation to accelerate during 2011-2013. The Iranian Central Bank acknowledged an inflation rate of 45% in July 2013, but many economists asserted that the actual inflation rate was 50% and 70%. The sanctions relief of the JPA helped reduce that to 20%. Some assert that inflation was fed by the policies of Ahmadinejad, particularly the substitution of subsidies with cash payments, rather than the effect of sanctions.

- *Industrial Production.* Because Iran's manufacturing sector relies on imported parts, the currency decline and financing restrictions have made it difficult for that sector to operate. Many Iranian manufacturers were unable to obtain credit and must pre-pay, often through time-consuming and circuitous mechanisms, to obtain parts from abroad. This difficulty is particularly acute in the automotive sector; Iran's production of automobiles fell by about 40% from 2011 to 2013. However, the JPA has benefitted the auto sector because of the sanctions easing on that sector required by the agreement. Still, press reports say that

---

[75] Clifford Krauss. "With Gas Byproduct, Iran Sidesteps Sanctions." New York Times, August 13, 2014.

[76] Rick Gladstone, "Data on Iran Dims Outlook for Economy," *New York Times*, October 13, 2012.

[77] Marjorie Olster, "Report: U.S. Sanctions Make Half Iran's Oil Income Out of its Reach," *Associated Press*, August 30, 2013.

manufacturing has rebounded only modestly since the JPA implementation began.

Iran's Mitigation Efforts

Prior to the JPA, Iran had mixed success mitigating the economic effect of sanctions.

Non-Oil Exports. Iran's primary strategy has been to substitute for crude oil sales by increasing sales of non-oil products. Some of the non-oil exports that have grown include minerals, cement, urea fertilizer, and other agricultural and basic industrial goods. The main customers for Iran's non-oil exports reportedly are countries in the immediate neighborhood, including Iraq, Afghanistan, and Armenia.

Oil Products Sales. Iran has sought to increase sales of oil products such as petrochemicals and condensates. Petrochemical sales are allowed under the JPA, and the JPA's cap on Iranian oil exports apparently does not include condensates either. Still, these exports have not come close to compensating for the loss of crude oil revenues.

Diversification and Developing Manufacturing Base. Arguing a position similar to that held by Supreme Leader Khamene'i, some economists have long maintained that Iran could best mitigate the effect of sanctions by diversifying its economy and reducing dependence on oil revenues and imported goods. Iranian manufacturers have increased production of some goods that Iranians are buying as they cut back on purchases of imported goods. In addition, some private funds are going into the Tehran stock exchange and hard assets, such as property. However, many of these trends generally benefit the urban elite.

Subsidy Reductions. In late 2012, in order to conserve funds, Ahmadinejad's government postponed phase two of his effort to wean the population off subsidies. That effort provided for cash payments to about 60 million Iranians of about $40 per month Iranians to compensate them for ending subsidies for commodities such as gasoline. Gasoline prices began to run on a tiered system in which a small increment is available at the subsidized price of about $1.60 per gallon, but amounts above that threshold are available only at a price of about $2.60 per gallon. Before the subsidy phase-out, gasoline was sold for about 40 cents per gallon. In April 2014, Rouhani raised gasoline prices further and began to reverse the Ahmadinejad approach entirely by limiting the cash payments to only those families who could claim financial hardship.

Import Restrictions. To conserve hard currency, Iran has reduced the supply of hard currency to importers of luxury goods, such as cars or cellphones (the last two of the government's 10 categories of imports, ranked by importance)—conserving its supply for the purchase of essential imports. Iranian importers of essential goods were able to obtain dollars at the official "reference" rate of 12,260 to the dollar, although the regime reportedly raised that rate to about 28,000 to the dollar in late June 2013—closer to the free market rate.

Effect on Energy Sector Long-Term Development

Sanctions have been intended to reduce Iran's production capacity over the longer term, taking advantage of the fact that Iran's oil fields are aging and in need of outside technology and investment to maintain, let alone boost, production. U.S. officials estimated in 2011 that Iran had lost $60 billion in investment in the sector as numerous major firms have announced pullouts from some of their Iran projects, declined to make further investments, or resold their investments to other companies. Iran says it needs $130-$145 billion in new investment by 2020 to keep oil production capacity from falling.[78] Iranian energy officials add that continued development of the large South Pars gas field requires $100 billion in new investment.[79]

Observers at key energy fields in Iran say there is little evidence of foreign investment activity and little new development activity sighted at various oil and gas development sites, as discussed in **Table 5**. However, the table also shows that some international firms remain invested in Iran's energy sector. Some of them have not been determined to have violated ISA and may still be under investigation by the State Department. As discussed above, some firms have avoided sanctions either through Administration waivers or invocation of the "special rule." No easing of sanctions on investing in Iran's energy sector is promised in the JPA, but there are numerous reports of international firms' talking with Iranian energy officials to plan for the possibility that this sanction will be lifted as part of a comprehensive nuclear deal. Iran is reportedly working actively to lure foreign investors back into the sector, including by hiring back many of the former officials that successfully negotiated such past investments.

Others maintain that Iran's gas sector can compensate for declining oil exports, although Iran has used its gas development primarily to reinject into its oil fields rather than to export. Iran exports about 3.6 trillion cubic feet of gas, primarily to Turkey and Armenia. On the other hand, sanctions have rendered Iran unable to develop a liquefied natural gas (LNG) export business. EU sanctions have also derailed several gas ventures, including BP-NIOC joint venture in the Rhum gas field, 200 miles off the Scotland coast, and inclusion of Iran in planned gas pipeline projects to Europe.

There has been a concern that some of the investment void might be "backfilled," at least partly, by Asian firms such as those from Malaysia, Vietnam, and countries in Eastern Europe. However, as shown in **Table 5**, many such "backfilled" deals remain in preliminary stages or themselves stalled as investors reconsidered whether to risk U.S. sanctions. Some of the backfill that has occurred has been conducted by domestic companies, particularly those controlled or linked to the Revolutionary Guard (IRGC). Foreign firms are reluctant to partner with IRGC firms as international sanctions have increasingly targeted the IRGC. The energy companies still active in Iran, particularly the Iranian firms, are reportedly not as technically capable as the international firms that have withdrawn from Iran.

---

[78] Khajehpour presentation at CSIS. Op. cit.

[79] Iran Faces Steep Climb to Join Gas Superpowers by 2017. *International Oil Daily*, April 29, 2014.

Table 5. Post-1999 Major Investments/Major Development Projects in Iran's Energy Sector

Date	Field/Project	Company(ies)/Status (If Known)	Value	Output/Goal
Feb. 1999	**Doroud (oil)** (Energy Information Agency, Department of Energy, August 2006.) Total and ENI exempted from sanctions on September 30 because of pledge to exit Iran market	Total (France)/ENI (Italy)	$1 billion	205,000 bpd
April 1999	**Balal (oil)** ("Balal Field Development in Iran Completed," *World Market Research Centre*, May 17, 2004.)	Total/ Bow Valley (Canada)/ENI	$300 million	40,000 bpd
Nov. 1999	**Soroush and Nowruz (oil)** ("News in Brief: Iran." *Middle East Economic Digest*, (MEED) January 24, 2003.) Royal Dutch exempted from sanctions on 9/30 because of pledge to exit Iran market	Royal Dutch Shell (Netherlands)/Japex (Japan)	$800 million	190,000 bpd
April 2000	**Anaran bloc (oil)** (MEED Special Report, December 16, 2005, pp. 48-50.)	Norsk Hydro and Statoil (Norway) and Gazprom and Lukoil (Russia) No production to date; Statoil and Norsk have left project.	$105 million	65,000
July 2000	**Phase 4 and 5, South Pars (gas)** (*Petroleum Economist*, December 1, 2004.) ENI exempted 9/30 based on pledge to exit Iran market	ENI Gas onstream as of Dec. 2004	$1.9 billion	2 billion cu. ft./day (cfd)
March 2001	**Caspian Sea oil exploration**—construction of submersible drilling rig for Iranian partner (IPR Strategic Business Information Database, March 11, 2001.)	GVA Consultants (Sweden)	$225 million	NA
June 2001	**Darkhovin (oil)** ("Darkhovin Production Doubles." Gulf Daily News, May 1, 2008.) ENI told CRS in April 2010 it would close out all Iran operations by 2013. ENI exempted from sanctions on 9/30, as discussed above	ENI Field in production	$1 billion	100,000 bpd
May 2002	**Masjid-e-Soleyman (oil)** ("CNPC Gains Upstream Foothold." MEED, September 3, 2004.)	Sheer Energy (Canada)/China National Petroleum Company (CNPC). Local partner is Naftgaran Engineering	$80 million	25,000 bpd
Sept. 2002	**Phase 9 + 10, South Pars (gas)** ("OIEC Surpasses South Korean Company in South Pars." IPR Strategic Business Information Database, November 15, 2004.)	LG Engineering and Construction Corp. (now known as GS Engineering and Construction Corp., South Korea)	$1.6 billion	2 billion cfd

Date	Field/Project	Company(ies)/Status (If Known)	Value	Output/Goal
October 2002	**Phase 6, 7, 8, South Pars (gas)** (Source: Statoil, May 2011) Field began producing late 2008; operational control handed to NIOC in 2009. Statoil exempted from sanctions on 9/30/2010 after pledge to exit Iran market.	On stream as of early 2009 Statoil (Norway)	$750 million	3 billion cfd
January 2004	**Azadegan (oil) – South and North** October 15, 2010: Inpex announced it would exit the Azadegan project entirely by selling its 10% stake; "special rule" exempting it from ISA investigation invoked November 17, 2010. China National Petroleum Corp. took a majority stake in South and North Azadegan fields in January 2009. However, on April 29, 2014, Iran cancelled the South Azadegan contract citing CNPC for performing "no effective work" since taking the stake in 2009. Industry sources say CNPC likely to also lose North Azadegan project also. (Iran-CNPC Breakup: Tehran Eyes the West, Christian Science Monitor, May 5, 2014.	Inpex (Japan) and CNPC (China)	$200 million (Inpex stake); China $2.5 billion	260,000 bpd
August 2004	**Tusan Block** Oil found in block in Feb. 2009, but not in commercial quantity, according to the firm. ("Iran-Petrobras Operations." APS Review Gas Market Trends, April 6, 2009; "Brazil's Petrobras Sees Few Prospects for Iran Oil," (http://www.reuters.com/article/idUSN03171107200090703.)	Petrobras (Brazil)	$178 million	No production
October 2004	**Yadavaran (oil)** Christian Science Monitor reports May 5, 2014, (op.cit.) that Iran says Sinopec has "experienced problems with regards to progress" on the field, which also extends into Iraq. But International Oil Daily quotes company on May 7, 2014, as saying project is on course to produce an initial 85,000 bpd by the end of 2014.	Sinopec (China), deal finalized Dec. 9, 2007	$2 billion	300,000 bpd
2005	**Saveh bloc (oil)** GAO report, cited below	PTT (Thailand)	?	?
June 2006	**Garmsar bloc (oil)** Deal finalized in June 2009 ("China's Sinopec signs a deal to develop oil block in Iran—report," Forbes, 20 June 2009, http://www.forbes.com/feeds/afx/2006/06/20/afx2829188.html.)	Sinopec (China)	$20 million	?
July 2006	**Arak Refinery expansion** (GAO reports; Fimco FZE Machinery website;	Sinopec (China); JGC (Japan). Work may have been taken	$959 million (major initial	Expansion to produce

Date	Field/Project	Company(ies)/Status (If Known)	Value	Output/Goal
	http://www.fimco.org/index.php?option=com_content&task=view&id=70&Itemid=78.)	over or continued by Hyundai Heavy Industries (S. Korea)	expansion; extent of Hyundai work unknown)	250,000 bpd
Sept. 2006	**Khorramabad block (oil)** Seismic data gathered, but no production is planned. (Statoil factsheet, May 2011)	Norsk Hydro and Statoil (Norway).	$49 million	?
Dec. 2006	**North Pars Gas Field (offshore gas).** Includes gas purchases Work crews reportedly pulled from the project in early-mid 2011. ("China Curbs Iran Energy Work" Reuters, September 2, 2011)	China National Offshore Oil Co.	$16 billion	3.6 billion cfd
Feb. 2007	**LNG Tanks at Tombak Port** Contract to build three LNG tanks at Tombak, 30 miles north of Assaluyeh Port. (May not constitute "investment" as defined in pre-2010 version of ISA, because that definition did not specify LNG as "petroleum resource" of Iran.) "Central Bank Approves $900 Million for Iran LNG Project." Tehran Times, June 13, 2009.	Daelim (S. Korea)	$320 million	200,000 ton capacity
Feb. 2007	**Phase 13, 14—South Pars (gas)** Deadline to finalize as May 20, 2009, apparently not met; firms submitted revised proposals to Iran in June 2009. (http://www.rigzone.com/news/article.asp?a_id=77040&hmpn=1.) State Department said on September 30, 2010, that Royal Dutch Shell and Repsol will not pursue this project any further	Royal Dutch Shell, Repsol (Spain)	$4.3 billion	?
March 2007	**Esfahan refinery upgrade** ("Daelim, Others to Upgrade Iran's Esfahan Refinery." *Chemical News and Intelligence*, March 19, 2007.)	Daelim (S. Korea)		NA
July 2007	**Phase 22, 23, 24—South Pars (gas)** Pipeline to transport Iranian gas to Turkey, and on to Europe and building three power plants in Iran. Contract not finalized to date.	Turkish Petroleum Company (TPAO)	$12. billion	2 billion cfd
Dec. 2007	**Golshan and Ferdowsi onshore and offshore gas and oil fields and LNG plant** contract modified but reaffirmed December 2008 (GAO reports; Oil Daily, January 14, 2008.)	Petrofield Subsidiary of SKS Ventures (Malaysia)	$15 billion	3.4 billion cfd of gas/250,000 bpd of oil
2007 (unspec.)	**Jofeir Field (oil)** GAO report cited below. Belarusneft, a subsidiary of Belneftekhim, sanctioned under ISA on March 29, 2011. Naftiran sanctioned on	Belarusneft (Belarus) under contract to Naftiran. No production to date	$500 million	40,000 bpd

Date	Field/Project	Company(ies)/Status (If Known)	Value	Output/Goal
	September 29, 2010, for this and other activities.			
2008	**Dayyer Bloc (Persian Gulf, offshore, oil)** GAO report cited below	Edison (Italy)	$44 million	?
Feb. 2008	**Lavan field (offshore natural gas)** GAO report cited below invested. PGNiG invested, but delays caused Iran to void PGNiG contract in December 2011. Project to be implemented by Iranian firms. (Fars News, December 20, 2011)	PGNiG (Polish Oil and Gas Company, Poland)	$2 billion	
March 2008	**Danan Field (on-shore oil)** "PVEP Wins Bid to Develop Danan Field." Iran Press TV, March 11, 2008	Petro Vietnam Exploration and Production Co. (Vietnam)	?	?
April 2008	**Iran's Kish gas field** Includes pipeline from Iran to Oman (http://www.presstv.ir/detail.aspx?id=112062&sectionid=351020103.)	Oman (co-financing of project)	$7 billion	1 billion cfd
April 2008	**Moghan 2 (onshore oil and gas, Ardebil province)** Jan. 7, 2014, GAO report says INA has withdrawn from Iran.	INA (Croatia)	$40-$140 million (dispute over size)	?
-	**Kermanshah petrochemical plant (new construction)** GAO report cited below	Uhde (Germany)		300,000 metric tons/yr
June 2008	**Resalat Oilfield** (Fars News Agency, June 16, 2008) Status of work unclear	Amona (Malaysia). Joined in June 2009 by CNOOC and another China firm, COSL.	$1.5 billion	47,000 bpd
January 2009	**Bushehr Polymer Plants** Production of polyethelene at two polymer plants in Bushehr Province. GAO Jan. 7, 2014, report says Sasol has withdrawn from Iran.	Sasol (South Africa)	?	Capacity is 1 million tons per year. Products are exported from Iran.
March 2009	**Phase 12 South Pars (gas)**—Incl. LNG terminal construction and Farsi Block gas field/Farzad-B bloc. Jan.7, 2014, GAO reports says ONGC Videsh has withdrawn from Iran, but project continued by NIOC subsidiary Petropars. Field began producing in March 2014.	Taken over by Indian firms (ONGC Videsh, Oil India Ltd., India Oil Corp. Ltd. in 2007); may also include minor stakes by Sonanagol (Angola) and PDVSA (Venezuela)..	$8 billion from Indian firms/$1.5 billion Sonangol/$780 million PDVSA	20 million tonnes of LNG annually by 2012
August 2009	**Abadan refinery** Upgrade and expansion; building a new refinery at Hormuz on the Persian Gulf coast	Sinopec	up to $6 billion if new refinery is built	

Date	Field/Project	Company(ies)/Status (If Known)	Value	Output/Goal
Oct. 2009	**South Pars Gas Field—Phases 6-8, Gas Sweetening Plant** CRS conversation with Embassy of S. Korea in Washington, D.C, July 2010 Contract signed but then abrogated by S. Korean firm	G and S Engineering and Construction (South Korea)	$1.4 billion	
Nov. 2009	**South Pars: Phase 12—Part 2 and Part 3** ("Italy, South Korea To Develop South Pars Phase 12." Press TV (Iran), November 3, 2009, http://www.presstv.com/pop/Print/?id=110308.)	Daelim (S. Korea)—Part 2; Tecnimont (Italy)—Part 3	$4 billion ($2 bn each part)	
Feb. 2010	**South Pars: Phase 11** Drilling was to begin in March 2010, but CNPC pulled out in October 2012. (Economist Intelligence Unit "Oil Sanctions on Iran: Cracking Under Pressure." 2012)	CNPC (China)	$4.7 billion	
2011	**Azar Gas Field** Gazprom contract voided in late 2011 by Iran due to Gazprom's unspecified failure to fulfill its commitments.	Gazprom (Russia)		
Dec. 2011	**Zagheh Oil Field** Preliminary deal signed December 18, 2011 (Associated Press, December 18, 2011)	Tatneft (Russia)	$1 billion	55,000 barrels per day within five years

Sources: As noted in table, as well as CRS conversations with officials of the State Department Bureau of Economics, and officials of embassies of the parent government of some of the listed companies (2005-2009). Some information comes from various GAO reports, the latest of which was updated on December 7, 2012, in GAO-13-173R. "Iran Energy Sector"

Note: CRS has neither the mandate, the authority, nor the means to determine which of these projects, if any, might constitute a violation of the Iran Sanctions Act. CRS has no way to confirm the precise status of any of the announced investments; some investments may have been resold to other firms or terms altered since agreement. In virtually all cases, such investments and contracts represent private agreements between Iran and its instruments and the investing firms, and firms are not necessarily required to confirm or publicly release the terms of their arrangements with Iran. Reported $20 million+ investments in oil and gas fields, refinery upgrades, and major project leadership are included in this table. Responsibility for a project to develop Iran's energy sector is part of ISA investment definition.

Effect on Gasoline Availability and Importation

In March 2010, well before the enactment of CISADA, several suppliers announced that they had stopped or would stop selling gasoline to Iran.[80] Others have ceased since the enactment of CISADA. Some observers say that gasoline deliveries to Iran fell from about 120,000 barrels per day before CISADA to about 30,000 barrels per day immediately thereafter, although importation later increased to about 50,000 barrels per day. The GAO report of January 7, 2014, identified no foreign firms selling Iran gasoline between October 1, 2012, and November 7, 2013, suggesting

---

[80] Information in this section derived from Javier Blas, "Traders Cut Iran Petrol Line," *Financial Times*, March 8, 2010.

that a phaseout of gasoline subsidies has reduced demand for gasoline and that Iran has increased domestic production.

Table 6. Firms That Sold Gasoline to Iran

Vitol of Switzerland (notified GAO it stopped selling to Iran in early 2010)

Trafigura of Switzerland (notified GAO it stopped selling to Iran in November 2009)

Glencore of Switzerland (notified GAO it stopped selling in September 2009)

Total of France (notified GAO it stopped sales to Iran in May 2010)

Reliance Industries of India (notified GAO it stopped sales to Iran in May 2009)

Petronas of Malaysia (said on April 15, 2010, it had stopped sales to Iran)[81]

Lukoil of Russia was reported to have ended sales to Iran in April 2010,[82] although some reports continue that Lukoil affiliates are supplying Iran.

Royal Dutch Shell of the Netherlands (notified GAO it stopped sales in October 2009)

Kuwait's Independent Petroleum Group (told U.S. officials it stopped selling gasoline to Iran as of September 2010)[83]

Tupras of Turkey (stopped selling to Iran as of May 2011, according to the State Department)

British Petroleum of United Kingdom, Shell, Q8, Total, and OMV are no longer selling aviation fuel to Iran Air, according to U.S. State Department officials on May 24, 2011

A UAE firm, Golden Crown Petroleum FZE, told the author in April 2011 that, as of June 29, 2010, it no longer leases vessels for the purpose of shipping petroleum products from or through Iran

Munich Re, Allianz, Hannover Re (Germany) were providing insurance and re-insurance for gasoline shipments to Iran. However, they reportedly have exited the market for insuring gasoline shipments for Iran[84]

Lloyd's (Britain). The major insurer had been the main company insuring Iranian gas (and other) shipping, but reportedly ended that business in July 2010.

According to the State Department on May 24, 2011, Linde of Germany said it had stopped supplying gas liquefaction technology to Iran, contributing to Iran's decision to suspend its LNG program.

Some of the firms sanctioned by the Administration on May 24, 2011, (discussed above), may still be providing service to Iran, including PCCI (Jersey/Iran); Associated Shipbroking (Monaco); and Petroleos de Venezuela (Venezuela). Tanker Pacific representatives told the author in January 2013 that the firm had stopped dealing with Iran in April 2010 but may have been deceived by IRISL into a transaction with Iran after that time.

Zhuhai Zhenrong, Unipec, ZhenHua Oil, and China Oil of China. Zhuhai Zhenrong is no longer selling Iran gasoline, according to the January 7, 2014, GAO report (GAO-14-281R). ZhenHua, a subsidiary of arms manufacturer Norinco, supplied one third of Iran's gasoline in March 2010, but there is little information on supplies since.

Emirates National Oil Company of UAE has been reported by GAO to still be selling to Iran. Three other UAE energy traders, FAL, Royal Oyster Group, and Speedy Ship (UAE/Iran) may still be selling even though they were sanctioned as discussed above.

Hin Leong Trading of Singapore may still be selling gasoline to Iran, as might Kuo Oil of Singapore.

Some refiners in Bahrain reportedly may still be selling gasoline to Iran.

Source: CRS conversations with various firms, GAO reports, various press reports.

---

[81] http://www.ft.com/cms/s/0/009370f0-486e-11df-9a5d-00144feab49a.html.

[82] http://www.defenddemocracy.org/index.php?option=com_content&task=view&id=11788115&Itemid=105.

[83] http://www.defenddemocracy.org/index.php?option=com_content&task=view&id=11788115&Itemid=105.

[84] http://www.defenddemocracy.org/index.php?option=com_content&task=view&id=11788115&Itemid=105.

Humanitarian Effects/Air Safety

Humanitarian-related effects of sanctions have been noted in several sectors, and some of the sanctions easing in the interim nuclear deal are intended to mitigate these effects. Press reports have mounted since mid-2012 that sanctions are hurting the population's ability to obtain Western-made medicines, such as expensive chemo-therapy medicines, and other critical goods. Some of the scarcity is caused by banks' refusal to finance such sales, even though doing so is technically allowed under all applicable sanctions. Some observers say the Iranian government is exaggerating reports of medicine shortages to generate opposition to the sanctions. Other accounts say that Iranians, particularly those with connections to the government, are taking advantage of medicine shortages by cornering the market for importing key medicines.

Some human rights and other groups have suggested potential solutions. The JPA provides for the international community to provide enhanced financial channels for Iran to import medicines, although the exact mechanism for such facilitation remains unclear. It was reported in late July 2014 that the U.S. Administration had reached out to European medical firms and asked them to expedite sales of medical goods to Iran. The Administration reportedly cleared banks in Switzerland and Japan to process financing for the shipments.[85]

In the aviation sector, some Iranian pilots have complained publicly and stridently that U.S. sanctions are causing Iran's passenger airline fleet to deteriorate to the point of jeopardizing safety. Since the U.S. trade ban was imposed in 1995, 1,700 passengers and crew of Iranian aircraft have been killed in air accidents, although it is not clear how many of the crashes, if any, were due to difficultly in acquiring U.S. spare parts.[86] The JPA provides for new sales of civilian aircraft parts to address this issue and Boeing and GE have applied for and obtained licenses to make some spare part sales to Iranian airlines.

Other reports say that pollution in Tehran and other big cities has worsened because Iran is making gasoline itself with methods that cause more impurities than imported gasoline. As noted above, Iran's efforts to deal with environment hazards and problems might be hindered by denial of World Bank lending for that purpose.

Sanctions Easings and Debate Following November 24, 2013, Nuclear Deal

U.S. officials have said publicly that the JPA requires "limited, temporary, targeted, and reversible" easing of international sanctions. As noted above, the sanctions relief of the JPA has had only a modestly positive effect on Iran's economy. Critics of the JPA asserted that the easing of sanctions would ignite a process of sanctions unraveling, pointing in particular to a 100+ member French business delegation that visited Iran in the first week of February 2014. The delegation reportedly included representatives of such major French companies as Airbus, GDF-Suez, Renault, Alcatel, and L'Oreal.[87] However, U.S. officials testified on July 29, 2014

[85] U.S. Pushes to Expedite Some Humanitarian Shipments to Iran. WSJ.com, July 28, 2014.

[86] Thomas Erdbink, "Iran's Aging Airliner Fleet Seen As Faltering Under U.S. Sanctions," July 14, 2012.

[87] http://www.thedailybeast.com/articles/2014/02/24/lawmakers-warn-michelin-over-iran html.

(referenced above), that the sanctions regime there has not seen any significant decline in international compliance since JPA implementation began. However, the possible Russia-Iran oil deal, discussed above, would seemingly violate sanctions if concluded.

Temporary Sanctions Relief in the JPA

In summary, the JPA (including its extension to November 24, 2014) provides for the following sanctions easing.[88] The relief was estimated to provide Iran with about $7 billion in total sanctions relief for the six-month JPA period (January 20-July 20, 2014), and then another approximately $4.3 billion for the four-month extension until November 24, 2014.

- Iran's oil exports are to remain at the level of about 1 million barrels per day. This implies that Iran's current oil customers will not reduce their oil purchases from Iran "significantly" during the interim period—such reduction is a requirement to avoid sanctions on the banks of those countries under Section 1245 of P.L. 112-81. To avoid penalizing these oil buyers, the Administration has exercised waiver authority under Section 1245(d)(1) of the National Defense Authorization Act for FY2012 (P.L. 112-81) and Section 1244c(1) of the Iran Freedom and Counter-Proliferation Act of 2012 ("IFCA,"Title XII, subtitle D, of the FY2013 National Defense Authorization Act, P.L. 112-239); the Administration has said it will not impose sanctions on foreign banks under Executive Orders 13622, 13645, and 13382 and related regulations. Waivers of Section 302(a) of the Iran Threat Reduction and Syria Human Rights Act of 2012 (P.L. 112-158) and of Section 5(A)(7) of the Iran Sanctions Act (P.L. 104-172, as amended) have been issued to permit transactions with Iran's national oil company (NIOC). The European Union has based its own regulations to allow shipping insurers to provide insurance for ships carrying oil from Iran.[89] *It should be noted that the waivers and sanctions suspensions under the JPA do not permit U.S. companies trading in such goods with Iran, but rather suspend U.S. sanctions on foreign companies that trade in such goods with Iran.*

- Iran was able to repatriate about $4.2 billion in oil sales proceeds during the first six-month JPA period, and will repatriate $2.8 billion for the four-month extension period. Iran is also able to use an additional $400 million of oil earnings to make tuition payments for Iranian students abroad (and another $300 million for the four-month extension period). Under the agreed JPA implementation plan, Iran accesses the hard currency in installments of $500 million or $450 million. The schedule was initially programmed to ensure that Iran completes at least the early stages of implementation, including diluting its 20% enriched uranium, before too much of the funds are released. The waiver authority under Section 1245(d)(1), discussed above, enables Iran to receive the oil proceeds installments directly.

- The JPA permits Iran to resume sales of petrochemicals and trading in gold and other precious metals, and to resume transactions with foreign firms involved in Iran's automotive manufacturing sector. The Administration estimates the value

---

[88] The Administration sanctions suspensions and waivers are detailed at: http://www.state.gov/p/nea/rls/220049 htm.

[89] Daniel Fineren. "Iran Nuclear Deal Shipping Insurance Element May Help Oil Sales." Reuters, November 24, 2013.

of the revenue Iran will accrue from these changes during the six months of the interim arrangement at about $2 billion, and for the four-month extension to produce an additional $1.3 billion in revenue. To enable these transactions, the Administration suspended application of Executive Orders 13622 and 13645, several provisions of U.S. trade regulations with Iran, and several sections of IFCA.

- The parties to the JPA pledged to facilitate humanitarian transactions that are already allowed by U.S. and partner country laws, such as sales of medicine to Iran, but which many banks refuse to finance. The United States also committed to license safety-related repairs and inspections inside Iran for certain Iranian airlines. Such licensing is specifically permitted under U.S. trade regulations written pursuant to Executive Order 12959 (May 6, 1995) and Executive Order 13059 (August 19, 1997) that impose a ban on U.S. trade with and investment in Iran. However, several Iranian airlines, including Iran Air, have been designated for sanctions under Executive Order 13382, which blocks U.S.-based property of entities designated as "proliferation supporters." To implement this commitment, the Administration issued a new "Statement of Licensing Policy" to enable U.S. aircraft manufacturers to sell the appropriate equipment to Iranian airlines and, as noted above, Boeing and GE have applied for such licenses. The Administration has suspended application of Executive Order 13382 and certain provisions of U.S. trade regulations with Iran to allow the supply of equipment to Iran Air. Steps to facilitate humanitarian shipments to Iran are discussed above.

- The P5+1 and Iran agreed to set up a Joint Commission whose tasks will include evaluating P5+1 compliance with its commitments for sanctions relief. The commission is empowered to consider Iranian complaints about foreign firms that Tehran believes have been sanctioned inappropriately for commercial interactions with Iran.

- The JPA requires that the P5+1 "not impose new nuclear-related sanctions," if Iran abides by its commitments under this deal, to the extent permissible within their political systems.[90]

Permanent Sanctions Easing?

A comprehensive nuclear deal between Iran and the P5+1 would include a broad easing of international sanctions against Iran. The JPA indicates that "nuclear-related" sanctions would be eased in a comprehensive deal, but in practice many sanctions are related to Iran's nuclear program even if they are not proliferation-related sanctions specifically. It is likely that Iran will demand easing of those sanctions imposed in recent years for the specific purpose of compelling Iran to agree to reduce the scope of its nuclear program. Iran is demanding the suspension or lifting of those sanctions imposed since 2010 that limit its oil and oil products exports, its use of the international financial system, and its receipt and repatriation of hard currency. Sanctions addressed purely at human rights and Iranian foreign policy will probably not be eased in a comprehensive nuclear deal.

---

[90] White House Office of the Press Secretary. "Fact Sheet: First Step Understandings Regarding the Islamic Republic of Iran's Nuclear Program." November 23, 2013.

As noted throughout this report, the Administration has substantial waiver and other authority to suspend application of sanctions on Iran. At the July 29, 2014, hearing referenced above, U.S. officials indicated that, if a deal is reached and Iran complies over a substantial period of time, the Administration might ask Congress to repeal or terminate those sanctions that cannot be lifted through Administration action alone. In a background briefing on the eve of March 17, 2014, talks with Iran on a comprehensive deal, a senior Administration official said

> we are doing a considerable amount of work, including consultations with the Congress, in that regard. We need to understand in great detail how to unwind sanctions and what—under what authorities and what can be done by the Executive Branch, what can be done by waivers, what will need congressional action.... any sanctions relief, should we get to a comprehensive agreement, will be phased in and will be in response to actions that Iran takes.[91]

The Administration has opposed attempts by some in Congress to link release of the $2.8 billion in hard currency during the JPA extension period to certification that Iran is not using those funds to support Hamas, Hezbollah, the regime of Asad of Syria, and other groups. Such linkage is proposed in S. 2667. Others in Congress have sought to provide for a congressional vote on any comprehensive agreement reached—a proposal the Administration has also opposed.

Possible Additional Sanctions

Should no comprehensive nuclear deal be reached and Iran resume pre-JPA nuclear activities, the Administration and many in Congress have indicated they seek to impose additional sanctions on Iran. The 113th Congress could decide to act on legislation already pending.

H.R. 850 and S. 1881

Two pending bills could affect the course of nuclear negotiations with Iran and could advance if negotiations on a comprehensive settlement break down. S. 1881, the "Nuclear Weapon Free Iran Act of 2013," was introduced on December 19, 2013. The operative provisions are similar to those of H.R. 850, a House bill that was passed 400-20 in July 2013, before the interim nuclear agreement.

- Both bills contain virtually identical provisions to require those countries that have exemptions allowing them to pay Iran's Central Bank for oil to accelerate their Iran oil import reductions to an aggregate cut of an additional 1 million barrels per day within one year of enactment. Countries that do not "dramatically reduce" their Iran oil buys would lose their exemptions.

- Both bills expand the proportion of the Iranian economy for which transactions are sanctionable (under IFCA; P.L. 112-239). H.R. 850 references the automotive and mining sectors; S. 1881 references the shipbuilding, construction, engineering, and mining sectors—defining them, along with the energy and shipping sectors, as "strategic sectors."

---

[91] Dept. of State. "Background Briefing on Next Week's EU-Coordinated P5+1 Talks With Iran." March 14, 2014.

- H.R. 850 authorizes, but does not mandate, sanctions for conducting financial transaction with Iran's Central Bank or other sanctioned Iranian banks for trade with Iran in any goods.

- Both bills would sanction foreign banks that help Iran exchange its foreign currency abroad—a provision identical to S. 892 (introduced on May 8, 2013).

- H.R. 850 would require the Administration to determine whether the Revolutionary Guard should be named a Foreign Terrorist Organization.

- S. 1881 contains provisions to delay the effective date of the sanctions beyond the duration of the interim nuclear deal (which expires July 19, 2014, based on implementation start on January 20). The sanctions contained in S. 1881 can be delayed for 180 days, provided the President certifies Iran is implementing the interim nuclear agreement, is negotiating in good faith on a final deal, has not (directly or through proxies) supported an act of terrorism against the United States, and has not conducted any tests of ballistic missiles of over 500 kilometer range. The suspension can be continued for an additional 60 days (two 30-day extensions) if the President certifies that a comprehensive deal that would "terminate" Iran's "illicit" nuclear program is imminent. The sanctions suspension would end if the President cannot submit a certification that Iran is fully implementing the interim nuclear deal. A waiver provision enables the President to forestall reinstatement of the act's sanctions.

- S. 1881 also provides for sanctions to be suspended if there is a final comprehensive nuclear agreement. The sanctions in the bill can be suspended for one year, with additional one-year periods, if the President certifies there is a final deal under which Iran agrees to dismantle its "illicit" nuclear infrastructure, is brought into compliance with U.N. Security Council resolutions, resolves all issues of possible military dimensions of its nuclear program, and permits constant monitoring of all "suspect" facilities in Iran. Under S. 1881, this sanctions suspension could be terminated if Congress enacts a joint resolution of disapproval. None of these delay provisions are contained in H.R. 850, which was passed by the House before the interim nuclear deal was reached.

Supporters of these bills have expressed mistrust of Iranian intentions, perhaps partly based on past nuclear discussions with Iran. Some Members say they doubt that the negotiating process will produce a result that ensures that Iran's nuclear program can only be used for peaceful purposes. Proponents of additional sanctions maintain that new sanctions could be useful in the negotiations by reinforcing to Iran that it would face consequences for failing to reach an acceptable comprehensive agreement. No legislation has been introduced, to date, to repeal or terminate sanctions against Iran if there is a permanent nuclear deal.

The Administration and outside critics of imposing new sanctions at this time argue that the enactment of any new sanctions legislation by Congress—no matter the effective date of the provisions—could split the international coalition that negotiated it. The Administration argues that some countries could end their cooperation with international sanctions if they perceive that the United States is not upholding the JPA pledge not to increase nuclear sanctions.[92] After the JPA was agreed, Iran's Foreign Minister Mohammad Javad Zarif said in an NBC interview that

---

[92] Ibid.

any U.S. imposition of new sanctions during the JPA period would void the deal. That Iranian position has been reiterated since the introduction of S. 1881. Other critics say that S. 1881 adds requirements to avoid new sanctions that are not in the interim deal—particularly that Iran not test new longer-range missiles. Others say S. 1881 imposes unattainable conditions on a final nuclear deal—that Iran's nuclear infrastructure be eliminated. Supporters of the bill say that the term "illicit" allows flexibility to allow Iran to continue some enrichment as part of a final deal. The President has said he will veto S. 1881 if it is passed by both chambers.

Another bill, H.R. 893, the Iran, North Korea, and Syria Non-Proliferation Act, has been introduced in the 113th Congress; it is primarily an update of an earlier law, discussed above, of virtually the same name. It contains a new provision that would mandate barring ships from porting in the United States if they had ported in Iran recently.

Other Possible U.S. and International Sanctions

There are a number of other possible sanctions that might receive consideration—either in a global or multilateral framework—presumably if the interim nuclear deal is not translated into a permanent deal and Iran continues to develop its nuclear program.

- *Sanctioning All Trade with Iran.* Some organizations, such as United Against Nuclear Iran, advocate sanctions against virtually all trade with Iran, with exceptions for food and medical products. The concept of a global trade ban on Iran has virtually no support in the United Nations Security Council, and U.S. allies strongly oppose U.S. measures that would compel allied firms to end commerce with Iran in purely civilian, non-strategic goods.

- *Comprehensive Ban on Energy Transactions with Iran.* Many experts believe that a U.N.-mandated, worldwide embargo on the purchase of any Iranian crude oil would put significant pressure on Iran. Even before the interim nuclear deal, the concept lacked sufficient support in the U.N. Security Council. Some advocate a U.N. Security Council ban on all investment in and equipment sales to Iran's energy sector. During the 1990s, U.N. sanctions against Libya for the Pan Am 103 bombing banned the sale of energy equipment to Libya.

- *Iran Oil Free Zone.* Prior to the EU oil embargo on Iran, there was discussion of forcing a similar result by closing the loophole in the U.S. trade ban under which Iranian crude oil, when mixed with other countries' oils at foreign refineries in Europe and elsewhere, can be imported as refined product. Some argue this concept has been mooted by the EU oil embargo, while others say the step still has value in making sure the EU oil embargo on Iran is not lifted or modified.

- *Mandating Reductions in Diplomatic Exchanges with Iran or Prohibiting Travel by Iranian Officials.* Some have suggested that the United States organize a worldwide ban on travel by senior Iranian civilian officials, a pullout of all diplomatic missions in Tehran, and expulsion of Iranian diplomats worldwide. The EU came close to adopting this option after the November 29, 2011, attack on the British Embassy in Tehran.

- *Barring Iran from International Sporting Events.* An option is to limit sports or cultural exchanges with Iran, such as Iran's participation in the World Cup soccer tournament. However, many experts oppose using sporting events to accomplish political goals.

- *Sanctioning Iranian Profiteers and Other Abusers.* Some experts believe that, despite the provision of P.L. 112-239 discussed earlier, the United States and international community should more aggressively target for sanctions Iranians who are exploiting special rights, monopolies, or political contacts for economic gain at the expense of average Iranians. Others believe that human rights sanctions should be extended to Iranian officials who are responsible for depriving Iranian women and other groups of internationally accepted rights.

- *Banning Passenger Flights to and from Iran.* Bans on flights to and from Libya were imposed on that country in response to the finding that its agents were responsible for the December 21, 1988, bombing of Pan Am 103 (now lifted). A variation of this idea could be the imposition of sanctions against airlines that are in joint ventures or codeshare arrangements with Iranian airlines.

- *Limiting Lending to Iran by International Financial Institutions.* Resolution 1747 calls for restraint on but does not outright ban international lending to Iran. An option is to make a ban on such lending mandatory. Some U.S. groups have called for the International Monetary Fund (IMF) to withdraw all its holdings in Iran's Central Bank and suspend Iran's membership in the body.

- *Banning Trade Financing or Official Insurance for Trade Financing.* Another option is to mandate a worldwide ban on official trade credit guarantees. This was not mandated by Resolution 1929, but several countries imposed this sanction subsequently. A ban on investment in Iranian bonds reportedly was considered but deleted to attract China and Russia's support.

- *Restricting Operations of and Insurance for Iranian Shipping.* One option, reportedly long under consideration, has been a worldwide ban on provision of insurance or reinsurance for any shipping to or from Iran. A call for restraint is in Resolution 1929, but is not mandatory. As of July 1, 2012, the EU has banned such insurance, and many of the world's major insurers are in Europe.

Table 7. Entities Sanctioned Under U.N. Resolutions and U.S. Laws and Executive Orders

(Persons listed are identified by the positions they held when designated; some have since changed.)

Entities Named for Sanctions Under Resolution 1737

Atomic Energy Organization of Iran (AEIO) Mesbah Energy Company (Arak supplier); Kalaye Electric (Natanz supplier); Pars Trash Company (centrifuge program); Farayand Technique (centrifuge program); Defense Industries Organization (DIO); 7th of Tir (DIO subordinate); Shahid Hemmat Industrial Group (SHIG)—missile program; Shahid Bagheri Industrial Group (SBIG)—missile program; Fajr Industrial Group (missile program); Mohammad Qanadi, AEIO Vice President; Behman Asgarpour (Arak manager); Ehsan Monajemi (Natanz construction manager); Jafar Mohammadi (Adviser to AEIO); Gen. Hosein Salimi (Commander, IRGC Air Force); Dawood Agha Jani (Natanz official); Ali Hajinia Leilabadi (director of Mesbah Energy); Lt. Gen. Mohammad Mehdi Nejad Nouri (Malak Ashtar University of Defence Technology rector); Bahmanyar Morteza Bahmanyar (AIO official); Reza Gholi Esmaeli (AIO official); Ahmad Vahid Dastjerdi (head of Aerospace Industries Org., AIO); Maj. Gen. Yahya Rahim Safavi (Commander in Chief, IRGC)

Entities/Persons Added by Resolution 1747

Ammunition and Metallurgy Industries Group (controls 7th of Tir); Parchin Chemical Industries (branch of DIO); Karaj Nuclear Research Center; Novin Energy Company; Cruise Missile Industry Group; Sanam Industrial Group (subordinate to AIO); Ya Mahdi Industries Group; Kavoshyar Company (subsidiary of AEIO); Sho'a Aviation (produces IRGC light aircraft for asymmetric warfare); Bank Sepah (funds AIO and subordinate entities); Esfahan Nuclear Fuel Research and Production Center and Esfahan Nuclear Technology Center; Qods Aeronautics Industries (produces UAV's, para-gliders for IRGC asymmetric warfare); Pars Aviation Services Company (maintains IRGC Air Force equipment); Gen. Mohammad Baqr Zolqadr (IRGC officer serving as deputy Interior Minister; Brig. Gen. Qasem Soleimani (Qods Force commander); Fereidoun Abbasi-Davani (senior defense scientist); Mohasen Fakrizadeh-Mahabai (defense scientist); Seyed Jaber Safdari (Natanz manager); Mohsen Hojati (head of Fajr Industrial Group); Ahmad Derakshandeh (head of Bank Sepah); Brig. Gen. Mohammad Reza Zahedi (IRGC ground forces commander); Amir Rahimi (head of Esfahan nuclear facilities); Mehrdada Akhlaghi Ketabachi (head of SBIG); Naser Maleki (head of SHIG); Brig. Gen. Morteza Reza'i (Deputy commander-in-chief, IRGC); Vice Admiral Ali Akbar Ahmadiyan (chief of IRGC Joint Staff); Brig. Gen. Mohammad Hejazi (Basij commander)

Entities Added by Resolution 1803

Thirteen Iranians named in Annex 1 to Resolution 1803; all reputedly involved in various aspects of nuclear program. Bans travel for five named Iranians.

Electro Sanam Co.; Abzar Boresh Kaveh Co. (centrifuge production); Barzaganin Tejaral Tavanmad Saccal; Jabber Ibn Hayan; Khorasan Metallurgy Industries; Niru Battery Manufacturing Co. (Makes batteries for Iranian military and missile systems); Ettehad Technical Group (AIO front co.); Industrial Factories of Precision; Joza Industrial Co.; Pshgam (Pioneer) Energy Industries; Tamas Co. (involved in uranium enrichment); Safety Equipment Procurement (AIO front, involved in missiles)

Entities Added by Resolution 1929

Over 40 entities added; makes mandatory a previously nonbinding travel ban on most named Iranians of previous resolutions. Adds one individual banned for travel—AEIO head Javad Rahiqi

Amin Industrial Complex; Armament Industries Group; Defense Technology and Science Research Center (owned or controlled by Ministry of Defense); Doostan International Company; Farasakht Industries; First East Export Bank, PLC (only bank added by Resolution 1929); Kaveh Cutting Tools Company; M. Babaie Industries; Malek Ashtar University (subordinate of Defense Technology and Science Research Center, above); Ministry of Defense Logistics Export (sells Iranian made arms to customers worldwide); Mizan Machinery Manufacturing; Modern Industries Technique Company; Nuclear Research Center for Agriculture and Medicine (research component of the AEIO); Pejman Industrial Services Corp.; Sabalan Company; Sahand Aluminum Parts Industrial Company; Shahid Karrazi Industries; Shahid Sattari Industries; Shahid Sayyade Shirazi Industries (acts on behalf of the DIO); Special Industries Group (another subordinate of DIO); Tiz Pars (cover name for SHIG); Yazd Metallurgy Industries

The following Revolutionary Guard affiliated firms (several are subsidiaries of Khatam ol-Anbiya, the main Guard construction affiliate): Fater Institute; Garaghe Sazendegi Ghaem; Gorb Karbala; Gorb Nooh; Hara Company; Imensazan Consultant Engineers Institute; Khatam ol-Anbiya; Makin; Omran Sahel; Oriental Oil Kish; Rah Sahel; Rahab Engineering Institute; Sahel Consultant Engineers; Sepanir; Sepasad Engineering Company

The following entities owned or controlled by Islamic Republic of Iran Shipping Lines (IRISL): Irano Hind Shipping Company; IRISL Benelux; and South Shipping Line Iran

Entities Designated Under U.S. Executive Order 13382
(many designations coincident with designations under U.N. resolutions)

Entity	Date Named
Shahid Hemmat Industrial Group (Iran)	June 2005, September 2007
Shahid Bakeri Industrial Group (Iran)	June 2005, February 2009
Atomic Energy Organization of Iran	June 2005
Novin Energy Company (Iran) and Mesbah Energy Company (Iran)	January 2006
Four Chinese entities: Beijing Alite Technologies, LIMMT Economic and Trading Company, China Great Wall Industry Corp, and China National Precision Machinery Import/Export Corp.	June 2006
Sanam Industrial Group (Iran) and Ya Mahdi Industries Group (Iran)	July 2006
Bank Sepah (Iran)	January 2007
Defense Industries Organization (Iran)	March 2007

June 2007

Pars Trash (Iran, nuclear program); Farayand Technique (Iran, nuclear program); Fajr Industries Group (Iran, missile program); Mizan Machine Manufacturing Group (Iran, missile prog.)

Aerospace Industries Organization (AIO) (Iran)	September 2007
Korea Mining and Development Corp. (N. Korea)	September 2007

October 21, 2007

Islamic Revolutionary Guard Corps (IRGC); Ministry of Defense and Armed Forces Logistics; Bank Melli (Iran's largest bank, widely used by Guard); Bank Melli Iran Zao (Moscow); Melli Bank PC (U.K.); Bank Kargoshaee; Arian Bank (joint venture between Melli and Bank Saderat). Based in Afghanistan; Bank Mellat (provides banking services to Iran's nuclear sector); Mellat Bank SB CJSC (Armenia). Reportedly has $1.4 billion in assets in UAE; Persia International Bank PLC (U.K.); Khatam ol Anbiya Gharargah Sazendegi Nooh (main IRGC construction and contracting arm, with $7 billion in oil, gas deals); Oriental Oil Kish (Iranian oil exploration firm); Ghorb Karbala; Ghorb Nooh (synonymous with Khatam ol Anbiya); Sepasad Engineering Company (Guard construction affiliate); Omran Sahel (Guard construction affiliate); Sahel Consultant Engineering (Guard construction affiliate); Hara Company; Gharargahe Sazandegi Ghaem

Individuals: Bahmanyar Morteza Bahmanyar (AIO, Iran missile official, see above under Resolution 1737); Ahmad Vahid Dastjerdi (AIO head, Iran missile program); Reza Gholi Esmaeli (AIO, see under Resolution 1737); Morteza Reza'i (deputy commander, IRGC) See also Resolution 1747; Mohammad Hejazi (Basij commander). Also, Resolution 1747; Ali Akbar Ahmadian (Chief of IRGC Joint Staff). Resolution 1747; Hosein Salimi (IRGC Air Force commander). Resolution 1737; Qasem Soleimani (Qods Force commander). Resolution 1747.

March 12, 2008

Future Bank (Bahrain-based but allegedly controlled by Bank Melli)

July 8, 2008

Yahya Rahim Safavi (former IRGC Commander in Chief); Mohsen Fakrizadeh-Mahabadi (senior Defense Ministry scientist); Dawood Agha-Jani (head of Natanz enrichment site); Mohsen Hojati (head of Fajr Industries, involved in missile program); Mehrdada Akhlaghi Ketabachi (heads Shahid Bakeri Industrial Group); Naser Maliki (heads Shahid Hemmat Industrial Group); Tamas Company (involved in uranium enrichment); Shahid Sattari Industries (makes equipment for Shahid Bakeri); 7th of Tir (involved in developing centrifuge technology); Ammunition and Metallurgy Industries Group (partner of 7th of Tir); Parchin Chemical Industries (deals in chemicals used in ballistic missile programs)

August 12, 2008

Karaj Nuclear Research Center; Esfahan Nuclear Fuel Research and Production Center (NFRPC); Jabber Ibn Hayyan (reports to Atomic Energy Org. of Iran, AEIO); Safety Equipment Procurement Company; Joza Industrial Company (front company for Shahid Hemmat Industrial Group, SHIG)

September 10, 2008

Islamic Republic of Iran Shipping Lines (IRISL) and 18 affiliates, including Val Fajr 8; Kazar; Irinvestship; Shipping Computer Services; Iran o Misr Shipping; Iran o Hind; IRISL Marine Services; Iriatal Shipping; South Shipping; IRISL Multimodal; Oasis; IRISL Europe; IRISL Benelux; IRISL China; Asia Marine Network; CISCO Shipping; and IRISL Malta

September 17, 2008

Firms affiliated to the Ministry of Defense, including Armament Industries Group; Farasakht Industries; Iran Aircraft Manufacturing Industrial Co.; Iran Communications Industries; Iran Electronics Industries; and Shiraz Electronics Industries

October 22, 2008

Export Development Bank of Iran (EDBI). Provides financial services to Iran's Ministry of Defense and Armed Forces Logistics

Banco Internacional de Desarollo, C.A., Venezuelan-based Iranian bank, sanctioned as an affiliate of the Export Development Bank

Assa Corporation (alleged front for Bank Melli involved in managing property in New York City on behalf of Iran)   December 17, 2008

March 3, 2009

11 Entities Tied to Bank Melli: Bank Melli Iran Investment (BMIIC); Bank Melli Printing and Publishing; Melli Investment Holding; Mehr Cayman Ltd.; Cement Investment and Development; Mazandaran Cement Co.; Shomal Cement; Mazandaran Textile; Melli Agrochemical; First Persian Equity Fund; BMIIC Intel. General Trading

February 10, 2010

IRGC General Rostam Qasemi, head of Khatem ol-Anbiya Construction Headquarters (main IRGC corporate arm) and several entities linked to Khatem ol-Anbiya, including: Fater Engineering Institute, Imensazen Consultant Engineers Institute, Makin Institute, and Rahab Institute

June 16, 2010

- Post Bank of Iran

- IRGC Air Force

- IRGC Missile Command

- Rah Sahel and Sepanir Oil and Gas Engineering (for ties to Khatem ol-Anibya IRGC construction affiliate)

- Mohammad Ali Jafari—IRGC Commander-in-Chief since September 2007

- Mohammad Reza Naqdi—Head of the IRGC's Basij militia force that suppresses dissent (since October 2009)

- Ahmad Vahedi—Defense Minister

- Javedan Mehr Toos, Javad Karimi Sabet (procurement brokers or atomic energy managers)

- Naval Defense Missile Industry Group (controlled by the Aircraft Industries Org that manages Iran's missile programs)

- Five front companies for IRISL: Hafiz Darya Shipping Co.; Soroush Sarzamin Asatir Ship Management Co.; Safiran Payam Darya; and Hong Kong-based Seibow Limited and Seibow Logistics.

Also identified on June 16 were 27 vessels linked to IRISKL and 71 new names of already designated IRISL ships.

Several Iranian entities were also designated as owned or controlled by Iran for purposes of the ban on U.S. trade with Iran.

November 30, 2010

- Pearl Energy Company (formed by First East Export Bank, a subsidiary of Bank Mellat

- Pearl Energy Services, SA

- Ali Afzali (high official of First East Export Bank)

- IRISL front companies: Ashtead Shipping, Byfleet Shipping, Cobham Shipping, Dorking Shipping, Effingham Shipping, Farnham Shipping, Gomshall Shipping, and Horsham Shipping (all located in the Isle of Man).- IRISL and affiliate officials: Mohammad Hosein Dajmar, Gholamhossein Golpavar, Hassan Jalil Zadeh, and Mohammad Haji Pajand.

December 21, 2010

- Bonyad (foundation) Taavon Sepah, for providing services to the IRGC; Ansar Bank (for providing financial services to the IRGC); Mehr Bank (same justification as above); Moallem Insurance Company (for providing marine insurance to IRISL, Islamic Republic of Iran Shipping Lines)

May 17, 2011

Bank of Industry and Mine (BIM)

June 23, 2011

- Tidewater Middle East Company; Iran Air; Mehr-e Eqtesad Iranian Investment Co.

March 28, 2012

Iran Maritime Industrial Company SADRA (owned by IRGC engineering firm Khatem-ol-Anbiya, has offices in Venezuela); Deep Offshore Technology PJS (subsidiary of the above); Malship Shipping Agency and Modality Ltd (both Malta-based affiliates of IRISL); Seyed Alaeddin Sadat Rasool (IRISL legal adviser); Ali Ezati (IRISL strategic planning and public affairs manager)

July 12, 2012

- Electronic Components Industries Co. (ECI) and Information Systems Iran (ISIRAN); Advanced Information and Communication Technology Center (AICTC) and Hamid Reza Rabiee (software engineer for AICTC); Digital Medial Lab (DML) and Value Laboratory (owned or controlled by Rabiee or AICTC); Ministry of Defense Logistics Export (MODLEX); Daniel Frosh (Austria) and International General Resourcing FZE)—person and his UAE-based firm allegedly supply Iran's missile industry.

November 8, 2012

- National Iranian Oil Company; Tehran Gostaresh, company owned by Bonyad Taavon Sepah; Imam Hossein University, owned by IRGC; Baghyatollah Medical Sciences University, owned by IRGC or providing services to it.

December 13, 2012

Atomic Energy Organization of Iran (AEOI) chief Fereidoun Abbasi Davain; Seyed Jaber Safdari of Novin Energy, a designated affiliate of AEOI; Morteza Ahmadi Behazad, provider of services to AEOI (centrifuges); Pouya Control—provides goods and services for uranium enrichment; Iran Pooya—provides materials for manufacture of IR-1 and IR-2 centrifuges; Aria Nikan Marine Industry—source of goods for Iranian nuclear program; Amir Hossein Rahimyar—procurer for Iran nuclear program; Mohammad Reza Rezvanianzadeh—involved in various aspects of nuclear program; Faratech—involved in Iran heavy water reactor project; Neda Industrial Group—manufacturer of equipment for Natanz enrichment facility; Tarh O Palayesh—designer of elements of heavy water research reactor; Towlid Abzar Boreshi Iran—manufacturer for entities affiliated with the nuclear program.

December 21, 2012

SAD Import Export Company (also designated by U.N. Sanctions Committee a few days earlier for violating Resolution 1747 ban on Iran arms exports, along with Yas Air) for shipping arms and other goods to Syria's armed forces; Marine Industries Organization—designated for affiliation with Iran Ministry of Defense and Armed Forces Logistics; Mustafa Esbati, for acting on behalf of Marine Industries; Chemical Industries and Development of Materials Group—designated as affiliate of Defense Industries Org.; Doostan International Company—designated for providing services to Iran Aerospace Industries Org, which oversees Iran missile industries.

April 11, 2013

Babak Morteza Zanjani—chairmen of Sorinet Group that Iran uses to finance oil sales abroad; International Safe Oil—provides support to NIOC and NICO; Sorinet Commercial Trust Bankers (Dubai) and First Islamic Investment Bank (Malaysia)—finance NIOC and NICO; Kont Kosmetik and Kont Investment Bank—controlled by Babak Zanjani; Naftiran Intertrade Company Ltd.—owned by NIOC

May 9, 2013

Iranian-Venezuelan Bi-National Bank (IVBB), for activities on behalf of the Export Development Bank of Iran that was sanctioned on October 22, 2008, (see above). EDBI was sanctioned for providing financial services to Iran's Ministry of Defense.

May 31, 2013

Bukovnya AE (Ukraine) for leasing aircraft to Iran Air.

December 12, 2013

Several Iranian firms and persons: Eyvaz Technic Manufacturing Company; The Exploration and Nuclear Raw Materials Company; Maro Sanat Company; Navid Composite Material Company; Negin Parto Khavar; Neka Novin Officials Iradj Mohammadi Kahvarin and Mahmoud Mohammadi Dayeni; Neka Novin alisaes including Kia Nirou; Qods Aviation Industries (operated by IRGC, produces UAVs, paragliders, etc); iran Aviation Industries Organization; Reza Amidi; Fan Pardazan; Ertebat Gostar Novin

February 6, 2014

Ali Canko (Turkey) and Tiva Sanat Group, for procuring IRGC-Navy fast boats; Advance Electrical and Industrial Technologies (Spain), for procurement for Neka Novin; Ulrich Wipperman and Deutsche Forfait (Germany), and Deutsche Forfait Americas (U.S.) for facilitating oil deals for NIOC.

April 29, 2014

Karl Lee (aka Li Fangwei) and 8 China-based front companies: Sinotech Industry Co. Ltd.; MTTO Industry and Trade Limited; Success Move Ltd.; Sinotech Dalian Carbon and Graphite Manufacturing Corporation; Dalian Zhongchuang Char-White Co., Ltd.; Karat Industry Co., Ltd.; Dalian Zhenghua Maoyi Youxian Gongsi; and Tereal Industry and Trade Ltd.

Iran-Related Entities Sanctioned Under Executive Order 13224 (Terrorism Entities)

July 25, 2007

Martyr's Foundation (Bonyad Shahid), a major Iranian foundation (bonyad)—for providing financial support to Hezbollah and PIJ

Goodwill Charitable Organization, a Martyr's Foundation office in Dearborn, Michigan

Al Qard Al Hassan—part of Hezbollah's financial infrastructure (and associated with previously designated Hezbollah entities Husayn al-Shami, Bayt al-Mal, and Yousser Company for Finance and Investment.

Qasem Aliq—Hezbollah official, director of Martyr's Foundation Lebanon branch, and head of Jihad al-Bina, a previously designated Lebanese construction company run by Hezbollah.

Ahmad al-Shami—financial liaison between Hezbollah in Lebanon and Martyf's Foundation chapter in Michigan

October 21, 2007

Qods Force and Bank Saderat (allegedly used to funnel Iranian money to Hezbollah, Hamas, PIJ, and other Iranian supported terrorist groups)

January 16, 2009

Al Qaeda Operatives in Iran: Saad bin Laden; Mustafa Hamid; Muhammad Rab'a al-Bahtiyti; Alis Saleh Husain

August 3, 2010

Qods Force senior officers: Hushang Allahdad, Hossein Musavi,Hasan Mortezavi, and Mohammad Reza Zahedi

Iranian Committee for the Reconstruction of Lebanon, and its director Hesam Khoshnevis, for supporting Lebanese Hezbollah

Imam Khomeini Relief Committee Lebanon branch, and its director Ali Zuraik, for providing support to Hezbollah

Razi Musavi, a Syrian based Iranian official allegedly providing support to Hezbollah

December 21, 2010

Liner Transport Kish (for providing shipping services to transport weapons to Lebanese Hezbollah)

October 11, 2011 (For alleged plot against Saudi Ambassador to the U.S).:

Qasem Soleimani (Qods Force commander); Hamid Abdollahi (Qods force); Abdul Reza Shahlai (Qods Force); Ali Gholam Shakuri (Qods Force); Manssor Arbabsiar (alleged plotter)

October 12, 2011

Mahan Air (for transportation services to Qods Force)

February 16, 2012

Ministry of Intelligence and Security of Iran (MOIS)

March 27, 2012

Yas Air (successor to Pars Air); Behineh Air (Iranian trading company); Ali Abbas Usman Jega (Nigerian shipping agent); Qods Force officers: Esmail Ghani, Sayyid Ali Tabatabaei, and Hosein Aghajani

These entities and persons were sanctioned for weapons shipments to Syria and an October 2011 shipment bound for Gambia, intercepted in Nigeria.

May 31, 2013

Ukraine-Mediterranean Airlines (Um Air, Ukraine) for helping Mahan Air and Iran Air conduct illicit activities

Rodrigue Elias Merhej (owner of Um Air)

Kyrgyz Trans Avia (KTA, Kyrgyzstan) for leasing aircraft to Mahan Air

Lidia Kim, director of KTA

Sirjanco (UAE) for serving as a front for Mahan Air acquisition of aircraft

Hamid Arabnejad, managing director of Mahan Air.

February 6, 2014

Several persons/entities in UAE aiding Mahan Air (see above): Blue Sky Aviation FZE; Avia Trust FZE; Hamidreza Malekouti Pour; Pejman Mahmood Kosrayanifard; and Gholamreza Mahmoudi.

Several IRGC-Qods Force offices or facilitators involved in Iran's efforts in Afghanistan: Sayyed Kamal Musavi; Alireza Hemmati; Akbar Seyed Alhosseini; and Mahmud Afkhami Rashidi.

One Iran-based Al Qaeda facilitator (supporting movement of Al Qaeda affiliated fightes to Syria): Olimzhon Adkhamovich Sadikov (aka Jafar al-Uzbeki or Jafar Muidinov).

Entities Sanctioned Under the Iran North Korea Syria Non-Proliferation Act or Executive Order 12938

The designations are under the Iran, North Korea, Syria Non-Proliferation Act (INKSNA) unless specified. These designations expire after two years, unless re-designated

Baltic State Technical University and Glavkosmos, both of Russia	July 30, 1998
(Both removed —Baltic on January 29, 2010, and Glavkosmos on March 4, 2010)	
D. Mendeleyev University of Chemical Technology of Russia and Moscow Aviation Institute (Both removed on May 21, 2010)	January 8, 1999
Norinco (China). For alleged missile technology sale to Iran.	May 2003
Taiwan Foreign Trade General Corporation (Taiwan)	July 4, 2003
Tula Instrument Design Bureau (Russia). For alleged sales of laser-guided artillery shells to Iran.	September 17, 2003 (also designated under Executive Order 12938), removed May 21, 2010
13 entities sanctioned including companies from Russia, China, Belarus, Macedonia, North Korea, UAE, and Taiwan.	April 7, 2004
14 entities from China, North Korea, Belarus, India (two nuclear scientists, Dr. Surendar and Dr. Y.S.R. Prasad), Russia, Spain, and Ukraine.	September 29, 2004
14 entities, mostly from China, for alleged supplying of Iran's missile program. Many, such as North Korea's Changgwang Sinyong and China's Norinco and Great Wall Industry Corp, have been sanctioned several times previously. Newly sanctioned entities included North Korea's Paeksan Associated Corporation, and Taiwan's Ecoma Enterprise Co.	December 2004 and January 2005
9 entities, including those from China (Norinco yet again), India (two chemical companies), and Austria. Sanctions against Dr. Surendar of India (see September 29, 2004) were ended, presumably because of information exonerating him.	December 26, 2005

7 entities. Two Indian chemical companies (Balaji Amines and Prachi Poly Products); two Russian firms (Rosobornexport and aircraft manufacturer Sukhoi); two North Korean entities (Korean Mining and Industrial Development, and Korea Pugang Trading); and one Cuban entity (Center for Genetic Engineering and Biotechnology).	August 4, 2006 (see below for Rosobornexport removal)
9 entities. Rosobornexport, Tula Design, and Komna Design Office of Machine Building, and Alexei Safonov (Russia); Zibo Chemical, China National Aerotechnology, and China National Electrical (China). Korean Mining and Industrial Development (North Korea) for WMD or advanced weapons sales to Iran (and Syria).	January 2007 (see below for Tula and Rosoboronexport removal)
14 entities, including Lebanese Hezbollah. Some were penalized for transactions with Syria. Among the new entities sanctioned for assisting Iran were Shanghai Non-Ferrous Metals Pudong Development Trade Company (China); Iran's Defense Industries Organization; Sokkia Company (Singapore); Challenger Corporation (Malaysia); Target Airfreight (Malaysia); Aerospace Logistics Services (Mexico); and Arif Durrani (Pakistani national).	April 23, 2007
13 entities: China Xinshidai Co.; China Shipbuilding and Offshore International Corp.; Huazhong CNC (China); IRGC; Korea Mining Development Corp. (North Korea); Korea Taesong Trading Co. (NK); Yolin/Yullin Tech, Inc. (South Korea); Rosoboronexport (Russia sate arms export agency); Sudan Master Technology; Sudan Technical Center Co; Army Supply Bureau (Syria); R and M International FZCO (UAE); Venezuelan Military Industries Co. (CAVIM). (Rosoboronexport removed May 21, 2010.)	October 23, 2008.
16 entities: Belarus: Belarusian Optical Mechanical Association; Beltech Export; China: Karl Lee; Dalian Sunny Industries; Dalian Zhongbang Chemical Industries Co.; Xian Junyun Electronic; Iran: Milad Jafari; DIO; IRISL; Qods Force; SAD Import-Export; SBIG; North Korea: Tangun Trading; Syria: Industrial Establishment of Defense; Scientific Studies and Research Center; Venezuela: CAVIM.	May 23, 2011
Mohammad Minai, senior Qods Force member involved in Iraq; Karim Muhsin al-Ghanimi, leader of Kata'ib Hezbollah (KH) militia in Iraq; Sayiid Salah Hantush al-Maksusi, senior KH member; and Riyad Jasim al-Hamidawi, Iran based KH member	November 8, 2012

Entities Designated as Threats to Iraqi Stability under Executive Order 13438

Ahmad Forouzandeh. Commander of the Qods Force Ramazan Headquarters, accused of fomenting sectarian violence in Iraq and of organizing training in Iran for Iraqi Shiite militia fighters	January 9, 2008
Abu Mustafa al-Sheibani. Iran based leader of network that funnels Iranian arms to Shiite militias in Iraq.	January 9, 2008
Isma'il al-Lami (Abu Dura). Shiite militia leader, breakaway from Sadr Mahdi Army, alleged to have committed mass kidnapings and planned assassination attempts against Iraqi Sunni politicians	January 9, 2008
Mishan al-Jabburi. Financier of Sunni insurgents, owner of pro-insurgent Al-Zawra television, now banned	January 9, 2008
Al Zawra Television Station	January 9, 2008
Khata'ib Hezbollah (pro-Iranian Mahdi splinter group)	July 2, 2009
Abu Mahdi al-Muhandis	July 2, 2009

Iranians Sanctioned Under September 29, 2010, Executive Order 13553 on Human Rights Abusers

1. IRGC Commander Mohammad Ali Jafari   September 29, 2010

2. Minister of Interior at time of June 2009 elections Sadeq Mahsouli

3. Minister of Intelligence at time of elections Qolam Hossein Mohseni-Ejei

4. Tehran Prosecutor General at time of elections Saeed Mortazavi

5. Minister of Intelligence Heydar Moslehi

6. Former Defense Minister Mostafa Mohammad Najjar

7. Deputy National Police Chief Ahmad Reza Radan

8. Basij (security militia) Commander at time of elections Hossein Taeb

9. Tehran Prosecutor General Abbas Dowlatabadi (appointed August 2009). Has   February 23, 2011
indicted large numbers of Green movement protesters.

10. Basij forces commander (since October 2009) Mohammad Reza Naqdi (was
head of Basij intelligence during post 2009 election crackdown)

11. Islamic Revolutionary Guard Corps (IRGC)   June 9, 2011.

12. Basij Resistance Force

13. Law Enforcement Forces (LEF)

14. LEF Commander Ismail Ahmad Moghadam

15. Ministry of Intelligence and Security of Iran (MOIS)   February 16, 2012

16. Ashgar Mir-Hejazi for human rights abuses on/after June 12, 2009, and for   May 30, 2013
providing material support to the IRGC and MOIS.

Iranians Sanctioned Under Executive Order 13572 (April 29, 2011) for Repression of the Syrian People

Revolutionary Guard—Qods Force   April 29, 2011

Qasem Soleimani (Qods Force Commander)   May 18, 2011

Mohsen Chizari (Commander of Qods Force operations and training)   Same as above

Iranian Entities Sanctioned Under Executive Order 13606 (GHRAVITY)

- Ministry of Intelligence and Security (MOIS); IRGC (Guard Cyber Defense Command); Law Enforcement Forces;
Datak Telecom

Entities Sanctioned Under Executive Order 13608 Targeting Sanctions Evaders

- Ferland Company Ltd. for helping NITC deceptively sell Iranian crude oil

Designations on February 6, 2014, (persons or firms that facilitated deceptive transactions for or on behalf of persons subject to U.S. sanctions on Iran)

Three persons based in the Republic of Georgia: Pourya Nayebi, Houshang Hosseinpour, and Houshang Farsoudeh;
and eight firms owned or controlled by the three: Caucasus Energy (Georgia); Orchidea Gulf Trading (UAE and/or
Turkey); Georgian Business Development (Georgia and/or UAE); Great Business Deals (Georgia and/or UAE); KSN
Foundation (Lichtenstein); New York General Trading (UAE); New York Money Exchange (UAE and/or Georgia); and
European Oil Traders (Switzerland).

Entities Names as Iranian Government Entities Under Executive Order 13599

Designations made July 12, 2012:

Petro Suisse Intertrade Company (Switzerland); Hong Kong Intertrade Company (Hong Kong); Noor Energy (Malaysia); Petro Energy Intertrade (Dubai, UAE) (all four named as front companies for NIOV, Naftiran Intertrade Company, Ltd (NICO), or NICO Sarl)

20 Iranian financial institutions (names not released but available from Treasury Dept.)

58 vessels of National Iranian Tanker Company (NITC)

Designations on March 14, 2013:

Dimitris Cambis and several affiliated firms named in Treasury Dept. press release.

Designation on May 9, 2013:

Sambouk Shipping FZC, which is tied to Dr. Dimitris Cambis and his network of front companies.

Designations on May 31, 2013:

Eight petrochemicals companies were designated as Iranian government entities, including Bandar Imam; Bou Ali Sina; Mobin; Nouri; Pars; Shahid Tondgooyan; Shazand; and Tabriz.

Designations on September 6, 2013:

- Six individuals including Seyed Nasser Mohammad Seyyedi, director of Sima General Trading who is also associated with NIOC and NICO. The other 5 persons sanctioned manage firms associated with NIOC and NICO.

- Four businesses used by Seyyedi to assist NIOC and NICO front companies. Three are based in UAE: AA Energy FZCO; Petro Royal FZE; and KASB International LLC. The other firm is Swiss Management Services Sari.

Entities Sanctioned Under Executive Order 13622 (For Oil and Petrochemical Purchases from Iran and Precious Metal Transactions with Iran)

May 31, 2013:

- Jam Petrochemical Company for purchasing petrochemical products from Iran.

- Niksima Food and Beverage JLT for receiving payments on behalf of Jam Petrochemical

Entities Designated as Human Rights Abusers or Limiting Free Expression Under Executive Order 13628 (Exec. order pursuant to Iran Threat Reduction and Syria Human Rights Act)

Designations made on November 8, 2012:

- Ali Fazli, deputy commander of the Basij

- Reza Taghipour, Minister of Communications and Information Technology

- LEF Commander Moghaddam (see above)

- Center to Investigate Organized Crime (established by the IRGC to protect the government from cyber attacks

- Press Supervisory Board, established in 1986 to issue licenses to publications and oversee news agencies

- Ministry of Culture and Islamic Guidance

- Rasool Jalili, active in assisting the government's Internet censorship activities.

- Anm Afzar Goster-e-Sharif, company owned by Jalili, above, to provide web monitoring and censorship gear.

- PekyAsa, another company owned by Jalili, to develop telecom software.

Designations made on February 6, 2013:

- Islamic Republic of Iran Broadcasting (IRIB) and Ezzatollah Zarghami (director and head of IRIB)

- Iranian Cyber Police (filters websites and hacks email accounts of political activists)

- Communications Regulatory Authority (filters Internet content)

- Iran Electronics Industries (producer of electronic systems and products including those for jamming, eavesdropping

Designations on May 30, 2013:

- Committee to Determine Instances of Criminal Content for engaging in censorship activities on/after June 12, 2009.

- Ofogh Saberin Engineering Development Company for providing services to the IRGC and Ministry of Communications to override Western satellite communications.

Designation on May 23, 2014:

- Morteza Tamaddon for cutting mobile phone communications and harassing opposition leaders Mir Hosein Musavi and Mehdi Karrubi when Tamaddon was governor-general of Tehran Province in 2009.

Entities Designated Pursuant to Executive Order 13645

December 12, 2012 (all for providing material support to NITC)

- Mid Oil Asia (Singapore)

- Singa Tankers (Singapore)

- Siqiriya Maritime (Philippines)

-Ferland Company Limited (previously designated under other E.O.)

- Vitaly Sokolenko (general manager of Ferland)

April 29, 2014, (for connections to deceptive oil dealings for Iran)

- Saeed Al Aqili (co-owner of Al Aqili Group LLC)

- Al Aqili Group LLC

- Anwar Kamal Nizami (Dubai-based Pakistani facilitator, manages bank relations for affilates of Al Aqili and Al Aqili Group. Also works for Sima General Trading, sanctioned under E.O. 13599)

Author Contact Information

Kenneth Katzman
Specialist in Middle Eastern Affairs
kkatzman@crs.loc.gov, 7-7612

www.ingramcontent.com/pod-product-compliance
Lightning Source LLC
Chambersburg PA
CBHW080515290526
45790CB00006B/2175